POLITICS FROM BELOW

Essays on Subalternity and Resistance in India

POLITICS FROM BELOW

Essays on Subalternity and Resistance in India

Alf Gunvald Nilsen

AAKAR

POLITICS FROM BELOW:
Essays on Subalternity and Resistance in India
Alf Gunvald Nilsen

First Published 2017

ISBN 978-93-5002-500-0

Published by
AAKAR BOOKS
28 E Pocket IV, Mayur Vihar Phase I
Delhi 110 091
aakarbooks@gmail.com
www.aakarbooks.com

Designed by
Limited Colors, Delhi 110 092

Printed at
Mudrak, Delhi 110 091

For

Jaya and Vineet

Sister. Brother.

Comrades.

Contents

Acknowledgements

This book brings together several of my essays on subalternity and resistance in India. Chapter 1 was first published in Norwegian in *Agora* in 2009, and has been translated into English especially for this book by Laurence Cox. Chapter 2 originally appeared as a chapter in the volume *New Subaltern Politics: Reconceptualizing Hegemony and Resistance in Contemporary India,* co-edited by Srila Roy and myself and published by Oxford University Press in 2015. Chapter 3 was first published in *the Journal of Poverty* in 2013 and chapter 4 originally appeared as a chapter in *Staking Claims: The Politics of Social Movements in Contemporary Rural India,* co-edited by Uday Chandra and Daniel Taghioff and published by Oxford University Press in 2016. I am grateful to the publishers for permission to republish my writings in this work, to Aakar Books for their interest in the project, and to Laurence for his expert translation from Norwegian to English.

The writings in this book are all based on research that I have carried out in and on India over the past sixteen years. This work would not have been possible without the two people to whom the book is dedicated—Jaya Mehta and Vineet Tiwari. Over the years, Jaya and Vineet have gone out of their way to help me carry out my various projects in India. They have also taught me a great deal of what I can claim to know about the country, its political economy, and its social movements. In the process, I have been fortunate to gain two treasured comrades and friends—and, most importantly, a big sister and a big brother. I offer this book, therefore, as a small token of how dear they both are to me.

New York, September 2016

Introduction

During the spring months of 2016, Narendra Modi's regime seemed to have succeeded in bringing about an impressive surge of growth in the Indian economy: in late May, the Central Statistics Office reported that the country's GDP grew at 7.9 per cent during the first quarter of the year—up from 7.2 per cent the previous year. As the *Financial Times* noted, these growth rates meant that India had overtaken a crisis-struck China as the world's fastest expanding large economy and the globe's most dynamic emerging market (Mallet 2016). Speaking at the Bloomberg India Economic Forum in March this year, Modi confidently claimed that "India's economic success is the hard-won result of prudence, sound policy and effective management" (Krishnan and Antony 2016). A neoliberal agenda of enhanced market reform—coupled with a thinly veiled Hindu majoritarianism (Jaffrelot 2015) —was of course at the centre of the political programme that propelled the BJP to a stunning victory in the general election of 2014 (Ruparelia 2015). Thus, if taken at face value, the recent growth figures suggest that this agenda—an agenda that has been concretized above all in the Make in India campaign, which aims at attracting greater levels of foreign direct investment to the country—has indeed succeeded in bringing about the "*acche din*" (good times) that the electorate was promised during Modi's campaign (Harriss 2015).

However, the story is more complex than this. There are good reasons to doubt the integrity of the growth figures, and the Indian economy is still failing to create employment at a satisfactory rate (Guruswamy 2016; Chaudhuri 2016). Moreover, beyond these immediate concerns, it is also a fact that India's socioeconomic trajectory remains fundamentally unequal and uneven (Chakravarty 2016). As Jean Drèze and Amartya Sen (2013) have recently pointed out, India is falling behind its poorer South Asian neighbours in terms of basic social development indicators like infant mortality rates, life expectancy, mean years of schooling, and female literacy rates. This is only one of many manifestations of the ways in which neoliberal reform in the country has been skewed in favour of elite interests (Desai 2016). A majority of the population—53.8 per cent according to the Oxford Poverty and Human Development Initiative (OPHDI 2015: 1)—still lives in poverty. Whereas neoliberalization has engendered many new profit opportunities for propertied groups, persistent poverty combines with increasing inequalities to create a scenario of unequal and uneven development that particularly affects vulnerable groups such as Dalits, women, Adivasis, marginal peasants, and the working classes in India's countryside and vast urban informal economy (Breman 2016; Corbridge, Harriss, and Jeffrey 2012: Chapters 3 and 4; Corbridge and Shah 2012; Kohli 2012; Nayyar 2006; Parry 2014; Walker 2008). In other words, the developmental trajectory that is touted as a pathway to "good times" is in fact at the heart of the making of the structures of deprivation, stigma, and disenfranchisement that define subalternity in contemporary India.

Such structures of power are the subject of the essays that comprise this book. And so is the resistance of those groups who are adversely incorporated into them—a form of collective agency that I shall refer to as subaltern politics

(Nilsen and Roy 2015). It is imperative to remind ourselves that despite the BJP's electoral victory of 2014, the hegemony of India's dominant social forces is far from an accomplished state of affairs. Quite the contrary: neoliberalization and Hindu majoritarianism are still contested in a number of ways—by the numerous land struggles unfolding across the nation's countryside; by subalterns who use their right to vote in oppositional ways, as they did in Delhi in 2014 and in Bihar in 2015; by youth protesting authoritarianism and casteism on university campuses; and by workers who challenge exploitation in new industrial belts and in the informal sector (Levien 2012, 2013; Palshikar 2016; Tripathy 2015; Tharu 2016; Ness 2015: Chapter 3; Agarwala 2013). It is of course true that many of India's social movements have entered into either abeyance or professionalization. Indeed, this is evidenced by the proliferation of NGOs in the country and the fact that recent progressive legal reforms in India have been won not by mass-based social movements but by "NGOs and advocacy groups, drawing on transnational networks, led by middle class intellectuals" (Harriss 2011: 138). Yet, as Srila Roy (2014, 2015) has shown in the case of feminist mobilization, this does not foreclose the continuous emergence of new oppositional political subjectivities. Similarly, the turn to law and "judicialized activism" in India does not necessarily herald "the *end* of politics but rather its transformation into a *righteous and rightful* form" (Bornstein and Sharma 2016: 87; see also Ruparelia 2013).

If critical scholarship is to be relevant in this context—that is, if it is to produce knowledge that can be of some use to the pursuit of progressive social change—it is necessary that we reflect on the logic of the theoretical optics that we bring to bear on the study of subalternity and resistance. In this book I do this through a sustained critical dialogue with the school of thought that has arguably done the most to direct scholarly attention towards the study of politics from below in India—namely the Subaltern Studies project. Regardless of the overwhelmingly historical focus of this project, it has, as Partha Chatterjee (2013: 49) puts it, "managed to scatter, reinvent and insert itself in several subsequent projects" and thus exercises considerable influence on the study of contemporary subaltern politics (see also Nilsen and Roy 2015). It is crucial, then, that we interrogate the conceptual templates that informed this project and ask critical questions about both their insights and their blind spots. In this book, I do precisely this through both conceptual discussions and analytical explorations.

I start by engaging the theorization of power and resistance in the Subaltern Studies project. My point of departure in the first essay is what I perceive to be a discrepancy between Ranajit Guha's seminal formulation of an agenda for the study of popular mobilization in India's struggle for independence and the actual dynamics that emerge from the empirical studies that were presented in the first six volumes of the series. As is well known, Guha's introduction postulated the existence of an autonomous domain of subaltern politics as the binary opposite of elite nationalism. I argue that, in contrast, studies by scholars such as Gyanendra Pandey, Shahid Amin, David Hardiman, and Swapan Dasgupta point towards a more porous boundary between elite and popular politics than what Guha's formulation suggests. I also problematize the ways in which this perspective has been reproduced in the study of contemporary social movements—in particular, struggles over land and other natural resources, such as water and forests—before moving on to propose an alternative theoretical approach for the study of subalternity and resistance. Drawing on the work of British Marxist historians such as E.P. Thompson and Antonio Gramsci's theorization of hegemony and subalternity, I develop a framework for critical inquiry into power and resistance in which the conception of autonomous domains give way to a notion of relational practices. Such a perspective, I argue, can enable us to come closer to the actual realities that subaltern groups confront and the ways in which they operate when they develop their oppositional projects. By developing such a perspective, we can open up a discussion about both the achievements and the limitations of such political practices—a discussion which in turn can play a role in the further development of "social movement projects" (Cox and Nilsen 2014) capable of rupturing institutionalized power relations and their forms of ideological legitimation.

The second essay deepens this theoretical engagement with a specific focus on state-society relations in the study of subaltern politics. I start by reviewing the ways in which the Subaltern Studies project has conceptualized the relationship between the state and subaltern groups in colonial and postcolonial India. Engaging with the work of Ranajit Guha, Partha Chatterjee, and Sudipta Kaviraj in particular, I call attention to the problems that attach to a persistently bifurcated view of state power and subaltern resistance. This perspective, I argue, flows from the problematic conception that subaltern resistance constitutes an autonomous domain, and fails to appreciate how subaltern groups have appropriated the institutions, discourses, and governmental technologies of the state in the enactment of collective resistance—both historically and in the present conjuncture. I then consider the view of the state that emerges from ethnographic studies of everyday forms of state-society relations that draw on Michel Foucault's notion of governmentality. I argue that these studies have been significant in bringing about a more relational conception of how subaltern groups in India conceive of and engage with the state. However, being grounded in a decentred and dispersed understanding of power, these perspectives do not engage sufficiently with the relationship between state formation and particular trajectories of capitalist development and the ways in which relations of class power both enable *and* constrain the pursuit of oppositional politics from below in and through the state. In the third part of the essay, I therefore present an argument for a historical sociology of state-society relations informed by Marxian understandings of state formation and state power. I draw on Gramsci's concept of "the integral state" as a point of entry to an analysis of the distinctive way in which the modern state mediates the construction of hegemony as an unstable equilibrium between subaltern and dominant groups. I fuse Gramsci's insights with Bob Jessop's concept of "strategic selectivity" in order to conceptualize the ways in which state power undergirds the reproduction of fundamental power relations in given social formations, and the constraints this imposes on subaltern politics in relation to the state.

There is a key unifying idea that underpins these two essays—namely that subalternity is both constituted and contested in and through hegemonic formations. On this reading, hegemony is not a monolithic form of ideological power imposed from above to produce an alignment of dominant and subaltern worldviews. Rather, it is a form of rule that is predicated—and here I am paraphrasing a Gramscian formulation that will figure prominently in what follows—on unstable equilibria of compromise that rest on composite equations of consent and coercion. And these equations have to be constantly negotiated—that is, new balances have to be struck between accommodation and repression of subaltern movements and their claims—in order to ensure the reproduction of hegemonic formations over time. Conversely, subalternity is neither a condition of passive subordination to a dominant order nor an autonomous form of insurgent otherness. To be subaltern is to be woven into material, institutional, and symbolic condensations of unequal social power relations. However, subaltern consciousness—as Gramsci was at pains to make clear throughout the *Prison Notebooks*—remains an unruly fusion of dominant ideologies and a "good sense" that negates the regnant order of things. The oppositional collective action of subaltern groups reflects this contradiction: it is articulated through appropriations of dominant practices, institutions, and idioms, yet also carries within itself the potential to transcend hegemonic forms of the political. Producing politically enabling knowledge revolves, to a considerable degree, around deciphering the dynamics of this mutual imbrication and reflecting carefully and critically about what it entails in terms of prospects for subaltern emancipation.

In the second part of the book I move on to present a set of analytical explorations that bring this perspective to bear on popular politics in contemporary India. I begin with a study of the Narmada Bachao Andolan (NBA, Save the Narmada Movement) that draws on my monograph *Dispossession and Resistance in India: The River and the Rage* (Nilsen 2010). I situate the Narmada dams in relation to the political economy of capitalist development in postcolonial India. Like Indian dam projects more generally, the Narmada dams projects are characterized by a distributional bias in favour of the country's "dominant proprietary classes" (Bardhan 1998). This distributional bias, I argue, must be understood in terms of how capitalist development in postcolonial India was brought about through a "passive revolution" (Kaviraj 1997) in which state-led development strategies resulted in the transfer of productive resources to propertied elites. I then trace and analyze the various phases of the Narmada anti-dam movement. I start by detailing the emergence of popular resistance to dispossession in the form of "militant particularisms" (Harvey 1996) that engaged the state in struggles for resettlement and rehabilitation in the dam-affected communities in Maharashtra, Madhya Pradesh, and Gujarat. The next phase of the movement witnessed the building of a pan-state campaign against dam-building on the Narmada river. In my analysis of this phase, I unearth the processes that led to the formation of the campaign as well as its internal frictions, and then discuss its trajectory from 1990 to 2000 with a particular focus on its engagements with the state apparatus across this ten-year period. In the final part of the essay, I turn to a detailed interrogation of the NBA's wider counterhegemonic project for alternative development. I show how the project was articulated through an appropriation of key idioms of national liberation and postcolonial nation-building rather than as an outright rejection of the idea of development. I move to discuss the contradictions that flowed from the fact that this project was articulated as an "oppositional populism" (Gupta 1998) and show how it was inadequately grounded in activist lifeworlds. I conclude by reflecting on the strategic lessons that can be drawn from the trajectory of the Narmada struggle for social movements in contemporary India.

The last essay in this collection focuses on Adivasi subalternity and resistance. In contrast to much writing on Adivasi politics in India today, which tends to focus on the Naxalite movement in central and eastern India and resistance against large-scale processes of dispossession, this essay focuses on democratic mobilization by Bhil Adivasis in western Madhya Pradesh against what I call the everyday tyranny of the local state. I begin with a brief recapitulation of the theoretical orientations that inform my approach to the analysis of state-society relations and subaltern politics in this region, and then move on to present a detailed account of the workings of the everyday tyranny of the local state in Bhil communities in the region. I locate the origins of this state-society relation in the making of "colonial state space"' (Goswami 2004) in the Bhil heartland during the 19th and early 20th century. I detail the ways in which this process eliminated the relationship of shared sovereignty that had existed between the forest polities of the Bhils and the tributary states of Hindu rulers in the region in the precolonial era, thus subordinating tribal communities to a state with vastly increased "infrastructural power" (Mann 1984). I then move on to present an analysis of the Adivasi Mukti Sangathan (AMS; Organization for Adivasi Liberation)—a movement that has been active in Badwani and Khargone districts since the early 1990s. My analysis delineates its significant achievements in terms of democratizing local state-society relations but also its encounter with brutal forms of state repression that ultimately quelled the movement. I conclude the essay by discussing the strategic relevance of understanding local mobilizational trajectories in relation to the contentious crafting of political macro-structures across historical time. I argue that the kind of victories that the AMS were able to win and the ways in which these victories democratized local state-society relations were crucial in terms of advancing a capacity for resistance in a context of extreme subordination. However, the very real impact of repression on the movement simultaneously suggests that it is necessary to work towards a counterhegemonic project that has the capacity to challenge existing power relations and their entrenched institutional manifestations.

Through these analyses I hope to contribute to advancing theoretically informed and empirically grounded debates about how the social movements of subaltern groups might carve out pathways to a more substantive democracy than the one that prevails in India today. The reason why it is necessary to have such debates was amply illustrated in the drama that unfolded in Gujarat as I was completing work on this book. In response to ever more brazen attacks by upper caste groups, Dalits organized an *azadi kooch*—a freedom march—from Ahmedabad to Una. As the march reached its destination on August 15—India's independence day—thousands of Dalits vowed to refuse stigmatizing work such as manual scavenging and disposing of dead cattle. Claims for recognition and dignity fused with calls for social justice as the emergent movement demanded that the state government distribute five acres of land to each Dalit family in Gujarat. "*Gay ki doom aap rakho; hame hamari jamin do!*"—"you keep the cow's tail; give us our land!" emerged as the key slogan directed against the BJP government and the Sangh Parivar more generally. This show of collective defiance happened in a state that for more than one and a half decades has been considered a stronghold of the neoliberalism and Hindutva majoritarianism that ascended to national power in the general elections of 2014. And significantly, it happened despite the fact that the Dalit movement has been perceived to be a waning force for a number of years. If there is much in the current conjuncture to fuel the pessimism of the intellect, then surely the capacity of subaltern groups to articulate and organize opposition against the odds should animate the optimism of the will. Moreover, it should also compel us to align our scholarly endeavours with those who challenge a hegemonic formation that has little in store for the vast majority of India's population but deepening marginality.

Part I

Theorizing Subaltern Politics

1

Autonomous Domains or Relational Practices?

Power and Resistance in Colonial and Postcolonial India

'The historiography of Indian nationalism has for a long time been dominated by elitism—colonialist elitism and bourgeois-nationalist elitism'. With this assertion Ranajit Guha (1982: 1) announced the arrrival of a new and fundamentally oppositional historiographical perspective which would become foundational for a whole school of studies of political protest and social movements in historical and contemporary India. The assertion opens his essay 'On Some Aspects of the Historiography of Colonial India', printed in the first volume of the *Subaltern Studies* series; the series title also gave its name to the project that was crystallizing in the work of Guha and his colleagues.[1]

Guha claims that this historiographical elitism, and its interpretation of the Indian struggle for independence from British colonial rule, was in reality 'an echo of imperialism' (1989: 296). Within the established dominant perspectives in modern Indian history—often referred to as the Cambridge school—the independence movement was viewed as a political project within which Indian elites, schooled through their participation in the colonial power's academic, bureaucratic and political institutions and motivated by the 'rewards' that national independence would bring in the form of material wealth, social status and political influence, mobilized large social groups around liberal-democratic demands for the transfer of power and Indian self-government. The problem with this perspective, according to Guha, is not only its implicit or explicit celebration of colonialism and its effects, but that the involvement of the 'subaltern' majorities in the independence struggle is portrayed as a passive response to mobilization from above, typically based on vertical ties of loyalty to the dominant elites, rather than as an expression of these groups' autonomous political consciousness and repertoires of action.

It is precisely this elitism that the Subaltern Studies group seeks to eradicate through studying subaltern groups' active resistance to oppression and exploitation under British rule. In opposition to the Cambridge school's perspective, Guha (1982: 4) asserts the existence of a 'politics of the people' constituting an autonomous domain, parallel to and isolated from the elites' mental world and sphere of influence, which found expression in the countless uprisings and protest movements that developed among the small peasants and indigenous populations of the Indian village and among India's dawning urban proletariat[2] in the course of the nineteenth and the first half of the twentieth century. And it is these movements which constitute the main empirical subject[3] of the first five volumes of *Subaltern Studies*.[4]

The Subaltern Studies project was initially based theoretically on the intersection between British Marxist historiography, Antonio Gramsci's perspectives on hegemony and popular resistance, and the study of peasant movements in the colonial world (Ludden 2003, Chaturvedi 2000a). The goal of writing 'history from below' was drawn from the British Marxist historians' analysis of the bourgeois revolution in England and the transition to industrial capitalism (Manning 1996, 1999; Hill 1991; Hobsbawm 1965; Thompson 1968, 1971, 1975, 1978[5]). The assumption that subaltern political consciousness and repertoires of action constituted an 'autonomous domain' was taken from Gramsci's programme (1998: 52) for the study of what he called 'subaltern classes'.[6] The fact that Subaltern Studies largely concentrated on political protest among small peasants in the Indian village is tied to the re-orientation then taking place in the study of the role of peasant movements within anti-imperialist struggles: contemporary revolutionary transformations in China, Cuba and Vietnam forced new analyses of and debates on the political significance of the peasantry within the historical development of capitalism and its global expansion (Wolf 1969; Scott 1976; Alavi 1965; Hobsbawm 1973).

And it is precisely this last element which also points to the contemporary Indian context within which Subaltern Studies developed. At the end of the 1960s, India was drawn into the vortex of the 'global 1968', which in the postcolonial states of the South found its expression in new social movements that took aim at the institutionalized elite politics practised in these states (Watts 2001: 172). In India, this was expressed in the Naxalite movement's guerilla war against the Indian state from 1967 until the early 1970s (Banerjee 1984)[7] and in the growth of a series of militant movements and protest waves in the 1970s (Omvedt 1993; Basu 1987; Vanaik 1990; Katzenstein and Ray 2005)—on such a scale that the Ministry of Home Affairs in Delhi feared a revolutionary situation (Ludden 2003: 5). This in turn was closely tied to the collapse of the Nehruvian nation-building model, in the shape of economic stagnation and the breakdown of the Congress Party's political legitimacy and consensus formation mechanisms, culminating in the national state of emergency between 1975 and 1977 under the then prime minister Indira Gandhi (Frankel 2005; Corbridge and Harriss 2000).

From the mid-1980s, Subaltern Studies became part of global academic discourse, in particular within American contexts where debates on identity, otherness and power were on the agenda.[8] The project thus entered into dialogue with newer theoretical tendencies and political directions. History from below, Gramsci and peasant movements gave place to dialogues with Edward Said's analyses of orientalism, Foucault's studies of power and discipline, and Derrida's literary deconstruction.[9] Publications in the series became ever more strongly marked by theoretical debates about historiography in postcolonial contexts and analyses of discursive power in colonial situations.[10]

Although the debate around this turn is an important one, it lies outside the scope of this chapter. Here I have chosen to focus on the original understanding of subaltern politics as an autonomous domain, and on the analysis of the 'politics of the people' during the national independence struggle.[11] Furthermore, I will explore how this perspective has affected and been used in later studies of new social movements and oppositional politics in postcolonial India. In this context, I want to raise questions about the foundational proposition that subaltern politics constitutes an autonomous sphere. I will demonstrate how the empirical studies presented in the series point in other directions, in particular towards a more porous boundary definition between elite and popular politics than the theoretical formulations which laid the basis for Subaltern Studies would indicate. I also wish to demonstrate how the use of this perspective is problematic when it comes to understanding new social movements in India. I claim that even if binary conceptual oppositions can be useful for opening up new debates about power and resistance, they tend to constrain a more precise analysis of how power is encountered, challenged, blocked or appropriated through the resistance of subaltern groups (Cooper 2002: 255). Against this background, I return to the British Marxist historians and Antonio Gramsci to draw up some guidelines for a more sophisticated framework for understanding power and resistance in Indian history and contemporary society, wherein autonomous domains give way to relational practices. In conclusion, I will briefly discuss the political implications of developing this theoretical perspective.

Theoretical Orientations 1

Elitism in Indian Historiography

For Ranajit Guha, elitism within the dominant modes of Indian historiography is a continuation of British colonialism and its self-legitimation as a progressive and educational project. This understanding of British colonial rule was first expressed in what Guha calls colonial and neocolonial historiography, which was a history produced by British authors and institutions and their Indian 'imitators'. Later it was expressed in bourgeois nationalist historiography, produced by Indian writers and historians, albeit often with contributions from liberal western historians. Guha (1982) writes:

> Both these varieties of elitism share the prejudice that the making of the Indian nation and the development

> of the consciousness—nationalism—which informed this process, were exclusively or predominantly elite achievements.

In the colonial and neocolonial variant of elitist historiography, Indian nationalism is presented as 'a function of stimulus and response' (Guha 1982: 1), where nationalism was understood as a product of how Indian elites related to the institutions, opportunities and resources created by British colonial power. In this process, these elites learned how to act politically and thus aimed to take over these institutions when introducing national self-government. In the bourgeois-nationalist variant, Indian elites are presented as leaders who brought the Indian masses to freedom. Nationalism thus becomes an expression of the 'goodness' of the native elite, and is often expressed as 'a sort of spiritual biography of the Indian elite' (Guha 1982: 2). Both approaches suffer from the same blindness, Guha argues, namely that they 'fail to acknowledge, far less interpret, the contribution made by the people *on their own*, that is, *independently of the elite* to the making and development of this nationalism' (Guha 1982: 3).

In his essay 'The Prose of Counter-Insurgency', published in the second volume of *Subaltern Studies*, the criticism is extended. Here Guha argues that the presentation of peasant revolts in dominant Indian historiography—as spontaneous events—erases the insurgents' subjective experiences, motivations and forms of consciousness, and hence also the meanings that the insurgents ascribed to their own actions (1983b: 2–3). This applies both to the presentation of peasant revolts in British administrative reports and in later presentations by British academics, as well as in analyses produced by liberal or left-leaning Indian historians. The orthodox Marxist understanding of the history of the independence struggle is also affected by Guha's critique, since in place of analysing peasant insurgents' subjective and religious political consciousness it replaces the actual insurgent with an abstraction frequently titled 'Worker-and-Peasant' (1983b: 33).

Subaltern Resistance as an Autonomous Domain

In the dominant historical interpretation of the independence movement, Indian politics is exclusively a matter of the institutions created by the British, and of the political and administrative activities which they and their Indian 'pupils' took part in. According to Guha this is an 'un-historical historiography', which ignores the 'politics of the people':

> For parallel to the domain of elite politics there existed throughout the colonial period another domain of Indian politics in which the principal actors were not the dominant groups of the indigenous society or the colonial societies but the subaltern classes and groups constituting the mass of the labouring population and the intermediate strata in town and country—that is, the people. This was an autonomous domain, for it neither originated from elite politics, nor did its existence depend on the latter. (Guha 1982: 4)

The politics which had its source in this domain was traditional in the sense that it could be traced back to the precolonial period. However, it was not archaic but developed itself in relation to, and adapted itself to the changed conditions caused by, British colonialism.

While mobilization within the political domains of the elites had a vertical form, a mixture of British parliamentary organizational forms and Indian semi-feudal political institutions, mobilization within autonomous subaltern domains was horizontal, based on the traditional organization of territoriality and kinship. While elite politics was legalistic and controlled, popular politics was violent and spontaneous, and was expressed above all in peasant insurgency. The ideology which held these insurgencies together was marked by 'a notion of resistance to elite domination', and 'the experience of exploitation and labour endowed this politics with many idioms, norms and values which put it in a category apart from elite politics' (Guha 1982: 5).[12] Guha explains this autonomy as a result of the fact that neither the Indian bourgeoisie nor the Indian working class were able to establish themselves as the national leaders of a bourgeois-democratic or a proletarian revolution of the kind seen in Europe.[13] This autonomy is not absolute: in the history of the independence struggle there are examples of mutual influence between the two domains, due above all to the nationalist elite's attempts to integrate the struggles of the masses with their own project (Guha 1982: 6).

The theory of subaltern politics as an autonomous domain was also developed by one of the other central figures within the Subaltern Studies group, Partha Chatterjee (1982, 1983a), in two articles discussing the development of and relationship between different historical 'modes of power'. Here Chatterjee elaborates a theory of different 'modes of power' intended to elucidate the political cultures that grow from different modes of production—in other words, cultures connected to 'the question of rights or entitlements in society, of the resultant power relationships, of law and politics, of the process of legitimation of power relations'—and how these relate to one another in those historical periods where one mode of production gives way to another (1983a: 316).

Chatterjee develops a typology of three modes of power: (1) the communal mode of power, which grows from an egalitarian agrarian society where earth, forests and other resources are jointly owned, where individuals' rights and duties follow from their membership of the community, and where political authority is an effect of the village community as a whole; (2) the feudal mode of power, based on physical domination as a result of military conquest and subordination of another group, and where a ruling class demands a portion of the surplus produced by its subjects; and (3) the bourgeois mode of power, where rulership is secured through a class's ownership and control of the means of production, the production process and the exchange values which are produced, as well as through the separation of the state from civil society (Chatterjee 1982: 317–318).

In communal societies it is above all the need for defence against external threats that shapes the exercise of political authority. Chatterjee designates this form as 'peasant-communal' (1982: 31, 34–35). He argues that it is anchored in the concept of a community that cannot be reduced to isolated individuals, and which is fundamentally religious:

> The very nature of peasant consciousness, the apparently consistent unification of an entire set of beliefs about nature and about men in the collective and active mind of a peasantry is religious. Religion to such a community provides an ontology, an epistemology as well as a practical code of ethics, including political ethics. (Chatterjee 1982: 3)

In the transitions between different modes of production, communal and feudal modes of power come into contact with one another and feudal overlordship is established.

There thus develops a power relationship between feudal rulers and their subordinates, not only economically and materially through the extraction of surplus, but also politically and culturally, in the form of the ideological buttresses of feudalism. The dominant ideology legitimates the overlordship of the ruling class, but must simultaneously recognize that this class's power finds its limits in relation to its subordinates (Chatterjee 1983a: 338). In other words, in feudalism it is possible to determine principles as to what can be seen as 'legitimate revolt', and it is precisely this ideological ambivalence which explains why central symbols of feudal power were often the target of peasant attacks during insurgencies, both in the Indian middle ages and under British colonial rule (1983a: 338; Guha 1983a: Ch. 1).

With colonialism a new power relationship arises, shaped by two historical processes of development. Firstly, there is a gradual development of a formal state apparatus and institutionalized politics. This development is very important because the colonial power's state apparatus operated for a long time as a conglomerate of feudal and bourgeois modes of power. Secondly, a differentiation takes place within the peasantry, as a result of the colonial power's appropriation of surplus and the integration of agriculture into the global market economy. This forms the basis for a class of relatively well-off peasants and educated groups which takes an active part in organized politics within the colonial power's state apparatus (Chatterjee 1982: 17).

However, this does not mean that the unorganized politics based on the small peasants' communal ideology is extirpated and disappears. Colonial India was characterized by peasant movements which were grounded precisely in this ideology, and which existed side by side with the domain of organized politics, and at times the two domains slid over into one another and influenced each other (1982: 36-37). For Chatterjee, it is precisely the admixture of feudal and bourgeois modes of power, and the persistent elements of the small peasants' communal ideology, which create the empirical terrain that is to be mapped and analysed when studying subaltern politics.

Autonomous Domains?

Indian Nationalism and the Politics of the People

I will now highlight two key motifs which recur in the empirical analyses of the 'politics of the people' in and during the Indian independence movement, as presented in four contributions to *Subaltern Studies*. The first motif centres on how the politics of subaltern groups is anchored in a 'moral economy' (Thompson 1971)[14] which surrounds established socio-economic relationships and defines the normative aspects of the relationship between ruler and subordinate within these. A typical theme of the contributions to *Subaltern Studies* is to highlight how popular insurgencies and movements can be traced back to processes of change which followed India's incorporation within the colonial power's political economy, and which broke with subaltern expectations that elites should behave according to the 'rules' of the moral economy. The second motif has to do with the intersection between subaltern politics and elite politics in cases where (above all) the Congress movement supported subaltern movements—up to the point where the radicalism of the masses broke with the elites' focus on national unity—and how this process was marked by a dynamic where subaltern groups appropriated symbols, idioms and practices from elite politics and interpreted these in the light of their own experiences of oppression and hopes for change.

Gyanendra Pandey's (1982) essay 'Peasant Revolt and Indian Nationalism' explores the growth of protest movements among the small peasantry of Awadh, in what is now Uttar Pradesh, between 1919 and 1922. In January 1921, violent protests broke out among small peasants in Awadh, with large-scale demonstrations and collective acts of violence. This in turn was the result of a mobilization going back to 1919, whose underlying cause was a series of agrarian relationships that had developed in the region since it first came under direct British rule in 1856.

As a result of the establishment of British control in the area, the *talukdars* of the region—a group consisting of local kings and clan chiefs, bureaucrats and rich farmers—secured control over large portions of the agricultural land in return for regular tax payments and services linked to the maintenance of law and order. This had a negative effect on the region's small peasantry, who to a large degree lost their customary claim on land and subsequently ended up as poor tenant farmers or day labourers. This took place at the same time as the Awadh peasantry in general became ever more deeply indebted. When large-scale protests broke out in 1921, this was the outcome of a mobilization that had taken place between 1919 and 1920 with the formation of peasant associations—Kisan Sabhas—which sought and found support from urban nationalist groups.

In its early phase the Kisan Sabha movement was characterized by a marked traditionalism, both in its choice of methods—social boycott, a well-known phenomenon in local villages, and the caste-based solidarity groups which held the movement together—as well as the use of religious symbolism as a consistent feature of the mobilization. The movements' demands were also based on a traditional understanding of rightful and moral struggle where what was put in question was not the local class structure as such, but rather deviations from what was considered acceptable behaviour on the part of the dominant group (Pandey 1982: 171). This perspective was reflected in the demands which were formulated: it was understood and accepted that landowners could make rightful demands on their tenants, and that these should be respected, but appeal was simultaneously made to the landowners to protect the small peasants against the misdeeds of their officials and to re-establish a rightful social balance.

As the Kisan Sabha movement developed, its traditionalist characteristics were weakened. In 1920 a peasant congress was called in Ayodhya, where the movement's participants came into contact with activists from the Congress and Khilafat movements. This inspired the participants and gave the movement new symbols and slogans. These impulses thus became the object of collective reflection, discussion and, as Pandey formulates it, 'unexpected interpretations' (Pandey 1982: 177) when the peasants returned home from the encounter. A new goal was emerging: the landowners' behaviour, which was becoming ever more brutal, had to be stopped, and peasants began to exercise resistance by refusing to obey orders, but also by physical attacks on the landowners' property. In this phase of the movement, too, ever more day labourers and lower-caste groups joined the protests, and a far sharper critique of the shared interests of the colonial authorities and the landowners was developed. In some areas the movement announced that Swaraj (self-government) had been established.

At this point the Kisan Sabha movement lost its support from Congress, and the regional administration attempted to stop the movement, both by imprisoning the leaders and by changing the laws which set the framework for rent and fees on farmland. But the protests returned in the form of the yet more radical Eka (unity) movement in 1922, this time entirely without support from Congress politicians. A new set of demands was presented: the peasants were willing to pay rent for farmland, but rejected a series of unreasonable fees which the landowners also required; they refused to carry out forced labour without pay or to pay fees for the use of wells and pastures; finally, the peasants resisted illegal eviction from their homes and lands. It was by now clear that the traditional ties of loyalty between small peasants and workers on the one side and landowners on the other side had been dissolved—they no longer had any resonance in Awadh's social reality.

The Eka movement was ultimately crushed by the superior firepower of the administration, but Pandey (1982: 187-88) asserts that its ideological development bears witness to the presence of two completely different interpretations of Swaraj in the elite and subaltern political domains. For the elites, it was necessary to maintain an alliance both with India's class of landowners and the peasantry in order to succeed in the demand for national self-rule. For subalterns, this was a recipe for continued oppression after the ending of British colonial rule. Thus, Pandey claims, it transpired that small peasants in Awadh 'sensed more accurately than the urban leaders did, the structure of the alliance that held up the colonial power in UP and the range of forces that might combine to fight it' (1982: 190).

In Shahid Amin's (1984) essay 'Gandhi as Mahatma', one sees even more clearly how the reinterpretation of the symbols of elite politics became a symptomatic feature of subaltern politics. Amin focuses on how small peasants in Gorakhpur in Uttar Pradesh interpreted one of Mahatma Gandhi's speeches at a mass meeting in the region in 1921. This reinterpretation is very important since it formed part of the development of a popular protest movement which later that year attacked a police station in Chauri Chaura and killed several of the serving officers there. It is also important as a contrast to the Congress movement's perception of an appropriate division of roles in Gandhi's mass meetings, where the people should be thankful for being able to be in Gandhi's presence for a short while and receive his blessing, before returning back to their usual activities (1984: 18).

Gorakhpur was becoming ever more politicized in advance of Gandhi's visit. Landowners and local princes who mobilized in order to be re-elected as representatives in local councils found themselves exposed to resistance from below, from small peasants who experienced these figures as oppressors. Local activists presented the boycott of the elections, and subsequently also their participation in the Congress movement's non-cooperation campaign, as part of Mahatma Gandhi's spiritual biography. When Gandhi finally visited Gorakhpur, he was met by an enthusiastic mass public which had often defied the will of their landlords when they set off to hear him speak. What did they hear? Gandhi's speech emphasized six points: the importance of unity between Hindus and Muslims; the importance of people abstaining from initiating militant resistance on their own initiative; Gandhi's wish that people should practise temperance and chastity; a recommendation to lawyers to give up their practice, that state schools should be boycotted, and that official titles should be renounced; a recommendation that people should start to spin their own cotton cloth; and a promise of the imminent coming of self-government.

Amin claims that the discussions which followed Gandhi's speech did not take account of his negative recommendation that the people should abstain from engaging in acts of resistance on their own initiative, while his positive recommendation as to the behaviour he expected to see from his true adherents and disciples, and his promise of the imminent arrival of self-government, were interlaced so that the first would lead to the second. This in turn was interpreted within traditional religious horizons of understanding, and local newspapers began to report a series of stories about Gandhi's occult power which typically revolved around how people who defied Gandhi's recommendations on temperance and chastity, dared to doubt his power, or resisted his will more generally, were punished. People who followed his will or wishes were rewarded or benefited from miraculous events. Thus Gandhi's visit and speech in Gorakhpur had sown a seedling in the consciousness of local small peasants, which enabled them to imagine 'the turning of [their] world upside down [...] the possibility of the inversion of many of those power relations deemed inviolable until then [...]' (Amin 1984: 25).

This was also expressed in the use of Gandhi's name and message in political meetings and activities in Gorakhpur, not least in the popular interpretation of Gandhi's promise of Swaraj for India. For the small peasants in the area, Swaraj came to take on a millennarian meaning: self-rule represented a new and better time where the peasant population would enjoy minimal taxation and nominal rental costs. As the local mobilization process took on a more militant form in late 1921, the arrival of self-rule—in opposition to what the Congress movement was preaching at this point—became understood as something which was dependent on the abolition of the police's authority in the region. As Amin notes (1984: 51), several of the peasants who took part in the attack on Chauri Chaura said that they acted as they did in order to further Gandhi's Swaraj. At the same time, the slogan 'Gandhi Maharaj ki jai' was given a new meaning: rather than adhering to Gandhi's line of non-violence, this now became a slogan which signalled the small peasants' collective power as they attacked a local market or police outpost.

Throughout this whole process it is possible to see how subaltern groups take hold of symbols and messages from elite politics, interpret these in relation to their own horizons of understanding, and use these interpretations to legitimate actions which clash with the elites' political agenda. In Gorakhpur, the peasants found a legitimacy for their insurgency in what were supposedly Gandhi's orders, but, as Amin points out, their actions were rooted in 'what was popularly regarded to be just, fair and possible' (Amin 1984: 54).

Similar chains of events and motifs can be found in studies of Adivasi movements by Dasgupta (1985) and Hardiman (1984).[15] In the article 'Adivasi Politics in Midnapur', Swapan Dasgupta analyses the social-historical processes of change and political mobilizations between 1760 and 1924 in the northwest part of Midnapur district in Bengal, also known as Jungle Mahals. This area was originally a forest region populated by various Adivasi groups, as well as a proportion of Hindus from lower caste groups. The Jungle Mahals were formally subject to the Mughal kingdom, but the attempt to exercise actual political authority from above was not made. In 1760 the area fell to the East India Company, and the British agricultural property regime was gradually introduced in the Jungle Mahals. This set in motion processes of change which would shape a field of opposition between state, landowners and moneylenders on the one hand and the Adivasi population—fundamentally small peasants—on the other.

Towards the end of the nineteenth century the Jungle Mahals had been divided among several large landowners, with the European-owned Midnapore Zamindari Company (MZC) as a prominent new representative of the new owning class in the region. With new landowners and a more locally present colonial administration, together with a steady inflow of moneylenders from outside the Jungle Mahals, the traditional village organizations came under pressure as small peasants became increasingly indebted in order to pay rents, and as a result often lost farmland which had been mortgaged for loans. The pressure on Adivasi economic and living conditions was intensified when the railway between Bengal and Nagpur was built towards the end of the nineteenth century: Midnapur's forests thus acquired a commercial value which MZC was quick to exploit. In order for them to do this, legislation was introduced which made the Adivasis' traditional use of the forest and its resources illegal.

Resistance to this process was first expressed towards the end of the eighteenth century in local protests against the forced sale of properties belonging to traditional landowners who could no longer service their taxation requirements. Here the whole local society stood together across class barriers. By 1830 this resistance had developed from local protests to more general insurgencies against colonial rule, such as for example the Kol Adivasis' insurgency in 1831 and the Bhumij insurgency in 1832-1833. The small peasants' support for local chiefs in this period was an expression of their rejection of foreign authority and foreign rulers, as well as a defense of traditional ways of life and social organizing as a result of incomers—*dikus*, as they were called—offending against the Adivasis' moral economy (Dasgupta 1985: 118–119).

Between 1914 and 1918, while Midnapur was negatively affected by the Indian economic recession, Adivasi resistance flowered once more, this time in the form of plundering local markets. The initiative for these actions came from the Adivasis themselves, not the Congress movement. It was clear that the raids were conscious actions whose targets were chosen according to specific criteria, and that the Adivasi movement was growing at this point through incorporating new groups and new issues. This, claims Dasgupta, indicates that 'there is a pre-existing subaltern domain of politics with which the elite domain intersects' (1985: 124).

This intersection took place in 1921, when large-scale waves of insurgency washed over the Jungle Mahals and nearby areas as a result of large groups of small peasants rising in protest against the behaviour of the landowners. This coincided with the Congress movement's non-cooperation campaign, and Congress activists took an active part in the Jungle Mahals' protests. The Congress' activists targeted MZC and organized a strike of the company's workers. This subsequently developed into a powerful movement against MZC, which was ultimately forced to negotiate with the Congress activists. As Dasgupta (1985: 126-127) writes, there was no doubt that the Congress activists' participation at this point was important for the development of the protest movement among the Adivasis.

But at the very point when MZC was placed on the defensive, the Congress activists chose to take a line where they negotiated for a more humane approach from the landowners, rather than abolishing the land ownership regime as such—thus betraying the hope of the small peasants who took part in the movement. However, the Adivasis did not let the Congress activists' moderate line hold them back, and in 1922 and 1923 new raids on markets and insurgencies against the landowners broke out—not only against MZC but this time also against Indian landowners who restricted the Adivasis' use rights in the forest areas of the Jungle Mahals. The movement was ultimately weakened by Congress' winding-down of the non-cooperation campaign, but in Dasgupta's exposition this nonetheless bears witness to the strength of subaltern politics as an autonomous domain and the specific concept of justice that gave shape to subaltern resistance (1985: 135).

David Hardiman's (1984) article 'Adivasi Assertion in South Gujarat' covers a shorter period than Dasgupta's study of Midnapur, but explores many of the same processes and dynamics. At the centre of Hardiman's study is the Devi movement which took place in the Ranimahal region of southern Gujarat in 1922. The movement took the form of a spirit medium whose message was diffused to large crowds of followers from local Adivasi groups. The message was mediated by individual adherents who fell into a trance and abjured their audience to practise vegetarianism, temperance and purity, as well as to boycott the Parsis who acted as moneylenders in the region.

The Ranimahal region was settled by Adivasi groups in the course of the nineteenth century. The Adivasis were largely peasants, and their village societies showed only limited social differentiation. The dominant groups in the region were moneylenders from higher caste groups, as well as Parsis engaged in the sale of spirits. At the same time, the colonial authorities' bureaucrats demanded their pound of flesh in the form both of tax and of forced labour and bribes. The Parsis in this region often owned land in several villages, sold spirits on credit to the Adivasis all year round and took payment for this in the form of work on their farms and fields. The Parsis' situation was further strengthened when the colonial power introduced new alcohol legislation forbidding local brewing and distilling. Parsis were thus in a position to establish a total monopoly on the sale of spirits. The profits from moneylending and spirits were in turn invested in the purchase of farmland. In this process, the Adivasis soon became victims of their own ignorance of how market mechanisms worked, and moved from being landowners to tenants (Hardiman 1984: 201–204).

The colonial authorities viewed this development as a result of a lack of education among the Adivasi groups and thus began to establish primary schools in the Ranimahal region. The new schools made a breakthrough when a recognized representative of one of the Adivasi groups in the area decided to send his two sons there. The schools became ever more popular among the local population, and in turn proved to have an unexpected function in that they gave rise to a generation of young Adivasis—typically from somewhat better-off families—who worked amongst their own for social reform. The ground was therefore laid for the coming of the Devi movement.

In the Ranimahal region, the Devi movement expressed itself as a mass phenomenon that attracted large groups of adherents among the Adivasis. Through trance experiences it became possible 'to articulate the deep-seated sense of wrong and the aspirations shared by the mass of the Adivasis of South Gujarat' (Hardiman 1984: 211). Hardiman denies that the Devi movement can be understood as 'Sanskritization'—that is, the expression of a desire for incorporation into the caste system by taking on the customs of higher caste groups such as vegetarianism. Such a strategy would have been useless if it was not combined with an explicit political challenge directed against the class structure of the region. And this was precisely what the Devi movement was: a complex challenge directed against the dominant classes in the Ranimahal region (Hardiman 1984: 214). The movement represented a cultural synthesis where subaltern groups made use of the dominant groups' symbols of ritual purity, but selectively: the Adivasis rejected the values of their immediate oppressors—the Parsis—but appropriated symbolic capital associated with other dominant groups in the region. In this way they cut their ties of dependence on the Parsis, at the same time as creating an opening for dialogue with external progressive groups (Hardiman 1984: 218–219).

The Parsis rapidly understood where this could lead if the movement spread, and with the help of the state apparatus an attempt was made to suppress the movement. Urban nationalists from Baroda reacted to this and gave their support to the Adivasis. While Gandhi's followers had worked in the area since 1921 and made his message known to the Adivasis, this was the first step in a process which saw the Devi movement come into ever closer contact with Congress activists. A conference was organized where the Adivasis met Vallabhbhai Patel and Kasturba Gandhi, who entered into dialogue with the movement's spirit mediums. The conference was seen as very successful and as a symbol of the transition from an 'old' to a 'new' politics: mass meetings among the Adivasis in the Ranimahal region became more secular, the mediums transmitted admonitions furthering Gandhi's principles, and urban nationalists were often given leading roles in the movement. Those of Gandhi's followers who entered the movement attempted to modify it by insisting that the most important thing was to practice personal cleanliness, and they toned down the challenge to the Parsis' dominant position. This, however, was not accepted by the Adivasis. The boycott was maintained, but Gandhi's ideology and his followers became popular in the Ranimahal region.

The examples presented above are obviously only a small selection of the many and rich studies of subaltern participation in the Indian independence struggle that have been produced through Subaltern Studies, but they illustrate a consistent and representative tendency which also constitutes the core of my objection towards the project's approach to the study of power and resistance, namely that there seems to have existed a far larger and more integrated contact surface between the politics and culture of elites and subalterns than what the theoretical framework which the studies start from would indicate. This is true both for the subaltern relationship to the nationalism of the elites and for the understanding of the moral economy of subaltern groups.

Subaltern Studies aimed to formulate a critique of how subaltern participation in the independence struggle was presented as the expression of a more or less passive adherence to the nationalism of the elites. This has been effectively achieved in the studies under discussion, but at the same time I want to assert that we are also confronted with something far more than historical scenarios which saw a certain contact between two political domains as the result of elite attempts to intervene in and give direction to subaltern resistance, as Guha and Chatterjee formulated it in their original theoretical contributions to the project.

Small peasants in Awadh interpreted the nationalists' message of Swaraj as being identical with the end of the landowner system. Gandhi's message of non-violence, the importance of a pious way of life and the imminent arrival of self-government was converted to a legitimation for direct attacks on the institutions of state violence in Gorakhpur. Adivasis in Midnapur found strength and inspiration in the Congress movement's intervention in their struggle against resource robbery and the loss of rights. The Devi movement transmitted Gandhi's message as part of its struggle against the dominant position of the Parsis in the Ranimahal region: this is of course far more than passive adherence to the nationalism of the elites, but it is also a very different relationship between elite and popular politics than what one might assume from the postulate of autonomy.

If autonomy had been the defining feature of the politics of the people, and if this politics lay beyond the reach of elites, one would also expect that elites' political repertoire would be irrelevant for, and rejected by, subaltern movements in favour of a traditional, religious, and communal culture and ideology. However, the fact seems to be that subaltern groups actively and selectively appropriated political symbols and ideological elements from the elite domain, and that they adapted these creatively to their own experience of oppression and their own hopes of achieving changes in the social order through collective resistance. In other words, what Subaltern Studies shows above all is the processes through which subaltern groups rendered the nationalism of the elites understandable on their own terms, and relevant for their own situations, rather than showing the existence of an autonomous political domain among these groups.

In response to this critique it can of course be said that the contributors to *Subaltern Studies* modify the postulate of autonomy—both theoretically and empirically—by recognizing the existence of points of contact between elite and popular politics. However, I want to claim that rather than being the expression of a thought-out theoretical perspective, these modifications are primarily an expression of how difficult, not to say unsustainable, it is to maintain a diametrical analytical division between power and resistance, dominant and subaltern. Within the Subaltern Studies project, these points of contact are reduced to two different political cultures and two different social groups, between which a short-term external relation arises. This does not recognize that social movements are typically characterized by a struggle over the interpretation of cultural symbols which operate within a societal totality where dominant and subaltern groups are internally connected via material and semiotic structures (Steinberg 1994a, 1994b).

That it is indeed this perspective which is employed in the approach to the study of subaltern politics, and which gives rise to the difficulties encountered, can be clearly seen in Chatterjee's response to criticisms of the concept of autonomy in Subaltern Studies:

> When it is argued that the subaltern classes inhabit an autonomous domain, the implication is not that they are not dominated. On the contrary, it is precisely to conceptualize this domination as a relation of power that one must identify the autonomy of the subaltern classes. Domination must exist within a relation. The dominant groups, in their exercise of domination, do not consume

> and destroy the dominated classes, for then there would be no relation of power, and hence no domination. For domination to exist, the subaltern classes must necessarily inhabit a domain that is their own, which gives them their identity, where they exist as a distinct social form, where they can resist at the same time as they are dominated. It is only then that one can talk about domination as a relation, as a process, as a movement that emerges out of an opposition … The point is to conceptualize a whole aspect of human history as a history, i.e. as a movement which flows from the opposition between two distinct social forces. (Chatterjee 1983b: 59)

This argument seems to me to be based on a logical flaw, in the sense that it is hard to imagine how a subaltern group, whose cultural and political horizons of understanding are defined as an autonomous domain, will give its adherence to the dominant groups' ideologies, and hence subject itself to these groups' socio-cultural domination. It might seem that Subaltern Studies operates with precisely such a division between economic and physical domination on the one hand and cultural and political autonomy on the other, but this in turn gives rise to two other problems.

Firstly, if subaltern political consciousness and activity is formed within an autonomous domain, why is it then the case, as a number of contributions to the series clearly show (Chatterjee 1982: 35), that subaltern resistance expresses itself not only in the destruction of the power symbols of the dominant group but also in their appropriation? As O'Hanlon (2002: 155) and Sivaramakrishnan (2002: 224) point out, this indicates that the insurgents' subjectivity was constructed in relation to the symbols and signs which expressed elite authority. Secondly, if it is the case that subaltern groups do not adhere, at least in part or to some degree, to dominant ideologies, how can one then explain the relatively long periods where these groups do not mobilize in open resistance, but partly subject themselves to and partly collaborate with their oppressors?[16] If one accepts instead that subaltern groups do adhere to parts of the dominant groups' ideologies, and that this in turn entails periods when the social order is marked by stable power relations, attention turns to the process whereby subalterns come to develop an oppositional consciousness and practices in relation to these ideologies, and how this process is marked by active appropriation and interpretation of dominant ideological symbols, with the possibilities and limits that this brings for subaltern resistance.

This leads us to the problems with the concept of subaltern moral economy in Subaltern Studies. The fact that there is a moral economy which authorizes different groups' rights and duties, and which entails that the dominant groups' right to rule is recognized by subalterns so long as the rulers live up to their duties, is another example showing that the exercise of power by dominant groups is at least to some extent based on subalterns' acceptance of dominant ideologies. This is clearly evident in, among others, Pandey's study of the peasant movement in Awadh, which in its initial phase expressed acceptance of the landowners' social position and a series of demands that the latter made on small peasants. At the same time, the fact that there are limits for what is seen as the legitimate exercise of power, and furthermore the fact that a breach with this moral code is an important cause of resistance from below, points towards the fact that the boundaries between the horizons of understanding of elites and subalterns are fluid rather than watertight, and that in the encounter between the two there develop syntheses of elements from both sides. But if one looks more deeply, it becomes clear that it is not this understanding that forms the basis of the Subaltern Studies approach to moral economy.

In Chatterjee's presentation, it appears that the small peasant's communal ideology survives its encounter with the dominant groups' ideology intact. When subaltern groups engage in insurgency against their rulers, they are motivated by a religiously-justified code that constitutes and protects the community's unity and interests in relation to external groups. This is, as Chatterjee notes (1982: 35), a universal feature of subaltern collective action. As Sivaramakrishnan (2002: 224) has pointed out, this is symptomatic of how Subaltern Studies has understood the substance of subaltern consciousness and practice, as grounded on a set of unchangeable structures of meaning. In this approach there is a clear echo of Lévi-Strauss' theory of the timeless essence of mythology and its role as a horizon of understanding. The construction of oppositional discourses seems to follow a model where the loss of land, rights and status is interpreted and given meaning through traditional religious filters (Sivaramakrishnan 2002: 230–231).

The question which is put to one side here is how cultural traditions are constantly invented and reinvented, deconstructed and reconstituted in relation to processes of historical change and in the encounter with new cultural ideologies and symbols. When, for example, Pandey's study of the peasant movement in Awadh shows that the radicalization of this movement found expression in a crumbling away of traditional ties of loyalty between small peasants and landowners, it is precisely such questions that should be raised for students of subaltern politics. This is a problem for all the studies explored above. While the focus is on how subaltern groups interpret elite messages in a way that often conflicts with its official meaning, on the basis of traditional religious frames of references—for example, Amin's analysis of the subaltern interpretation of Gandhi's speech in Gorakhpur—it is rarely asked if this process also entails a reinterpretation of subaltern cultural traditions. Even in Hardiman's study of the Devi movement, where Adivasis drew on both elements of high-caste culture and the secular message of organized nationalism as part of a social reform strategy, what ultimately explains the movement's strength and spread is that it finds a religious resonance in subaltern mentalities (Sivaramakrishnan 2002: 229–230).

The analytical limitations that the view of subaltern politics as an autonomous domain sets to the study of power and resistance should now be relatively clear. It seems necessary to move towards a perspective which concentrates on power and resistance as relational practices, where the boundaries between dominant and subaltern political cultures are porous and fluid. This does not mean that we fall back on a vision of subaltern groups as passive participants in the political projects of elites, but that we think about subaltern resistance in a different way:

> ...it is the creative practice of the subaltern which now becomes the focus of our attention, his ability to appropriate and mould cultural materials of almost any provenance to his own purposes, and to discard those, however sacred or apparently an integral part of his being, which no longer serve him. (O'Hanlon 2002: 146).

The great need for such a reorientation becomes even clearer once we consider the problematic aspects of how perspectives from Subaltern Studies have been reproduced in studies of new social movements and subaltern politics in postcolonial India.

Autonomy in India's New Social Movements

The assumption of subaltern politics as an autonomous domain has had a strong influence on studies of the new social movements which developed in the 1970s in India. These movements often represented groups and issues which had been more or less marginalized by the Nehruvian nation-building project, and which had also not been represented by the established left parties in India—such as Adivasis and coastal fishing communities, feminism and environmental questions (Omvedt 1993). Academic studies often present these movements as if they operated in an autonomous political space, beyond a new form of elite politics that revolves around a modernist discourse of development and the liberal democratic politics of the state.[17]

One example of this is Parajuli's (1992) analysis of new social movements in India. He claims that these movements' political meaning consists in challenging the Indian state's development paradigm. The new social movements do this by formulating 'counter discourses' based on '[situated] knowledge that is locatable in time and space, embodied in struggle and participatory in process' (1992: 186, 185). With reference to movements which have challenged large dam projects, mining and modern logging in various parts of India, he argues that they have achieved a 'conceptual maturity and confidence to challenge the whole edifice of modern resource management and development' as they 'renew and reassert subjugated traditions of knowledge in a new situation' (Parajuli 1992: 32–33). Vandana Shiva and Maria Mies have claimed that women activists in the well-known Chipko movement 'expect nothing from 'development' or from the money economy. They want to pursue their autonomous control over their subsistence base, their common property resources: the land, water, forests, hills.' (cited in Rangan 2000: 34). Similarly, it has been argued that the movement against dam construction on the Narmada river in central India—Narmada Bachao Andolan—upholds 'the lived space of Adivasi and peasant communities' against the 'abstract space' of the state and transnational companies (Kala 2001: 14).

However, these perspectives have been challenged by detailed empirical studies of social movements which demonstrate that these movements challenge dominant discourses of development from the inside rather than rejecting them, and to integrate the state's democratic processes into their strategic repertoire of action. For example, Haripriya Rangan (1996, 2000) and Subir Sinha (2004) have both presented detailed studies of popular mobilization in the Tehri-Garwhal region in the Indian Himalayas—the birthplace of the Chipko movement of the 1970s—and both arrive at similar conclusions. The Chipko movement, which challenged commercial logging in the region, can be best understood as 'demanding their rights to greater access to a more generous idea of development' (Rangan 2000: 222). The modern development paradigm is used in the movement's practices and discourses as the starting point for articulating 'new political programmes' and creating 'new bases for social and political life' (Sinha 2004: 308). In my own research on the Narmada Bachao Andolan, I have shown how the movement found its starting point in a dialogue between Adivasi groups and activists from voluntary organizations who created a consciousness and form of practice centred around the demand that local state officials must respect Adivasis' political and civil rights; and furthermore, how the campaign against a wide-ranging dam project was expressed in a counter discourse which appropriated a range of symbols from the state's developmental ideology, centred on democratic participation and social justice, precisely in order to challenge this ideology's destructive consequences in practice for Adivasis and small peasants in the Narmada Valley (Nilsen 2007, 2008, 2010; see also chapter 3 of this book).

These aspects of India's new social movements indicate that national and transnational development discourses, as well as the nation-state's institutional apparatuses, democratic discourses and administrative procedures have been far more interwoven into subaltern groups' consciousness and practice than analyists like Parajuli would have it. Akhil Gupta (1998), for example, points out that the Indian nation-state's development ideology has become a central part of peasants' everyday social reality, *inter alia* through populist political programmes constructed by central authorities to legitimate their rule. This in turn has led to the development of an 'oppositional populism' where protest movements typically call state authorities to account for not living up to their own promises on generating progress. It is thus a matter of a struggle over 'the meaning and direction of development' rather than a refusal of India's postcolonial development ideology in its entirety (Gupta 1998: 74). Fuller and Harris furthermore underline the fact that 'the modern Indian state plays an important part in popular consciousness and understanding as well as in people's daily lives', and this means that 'even the poor, low-status and weak can sometimes benefit from their own adequately competent manipulation of political and administrative systems' (2001: 2, 25).

Partha Chatterjee (2004) has recently attempted to formulate a new perspective which takes account of this interweaving and of how it is expressed in subaltern politics in present-day India. Chatterjee's starting point is the fact that subaltern groups use the state's administrative population categories—categories which, for example, distinguish between caste groups with a right to reserved quotas in government jobs or which set an official poverty level and assign certain goods and rights to those who fall under this level[18]—within their everyday activities of resistance. This form of oppositional practice, which Chatterjee designates as the 'politics of the governed', originates in the postcolonial state's specific historical development process. In the west, the concept of citizenship developed from a set of civil and political rights which define civil society into a more complex set of social arrangements and forms of administrative regulation which constitute what can be called political society.

Postcolonial states, by contrast, are shaped by the fact that the state's forms of administrative regulation were introduced earlier than political and civil rights, as part of the authorities' attempts to establish power and directive capacity in the colonies. These forms of administrative regulation were continued by the postcolonial states; even if national independence also involved the introduction of civil and political rights, civil society remained a sphere of elite politics, marked by respect for democratic principles, legal frameworks and bureaucratic procedures. Subaltern groups operate within political society, where they set out their demands to public institutions as well as NGOs which are responsible for fulfilling the state's responsibilities to poor and marginalized groups. This field is characterized by a 'paralegal' dynamic, in that the state response to subaltern mobilization within political society often breaches legal statutes and bureaucratic norms (Chatterjee 2004: 73–75). The result is 'a constantly shifting compromise between the normative values of modernity and the moral assertion of popular demands' (2004: 41).

At first sight, Chatterjee's perspective might seem to be a far more flexible presentation of the dynamics within subaltern politics than can be found either in Subaltern Studies or in some interpretations of India's new social movements—which in turn can be seen as an expression of the recognition that the modern state has become an integrated part of popular consciousness and practice since Indian independence in 1947. But the idea of clear distinctions between elite and popular political domains also figures strongly in this perspective, in the form of the contrast Chatterjee draws between civil and political society. Indeed, a short overview of some studies of subaltern politics in present-day India shows that these two domains are not the watertight compartments that Chatterjee's analysis presents them as. Stuart Corbridge and John Harriss (2000: 200-227), for example, have shown how subaltern groups in India both make use of administrative population categories—for example, caste-based reservations for jobs—which constitute political society—and of the official political process which constitutes civil society, through participation in parties which represent low-caste groups and which in recent years have won power in several Indian states. This development breaks the monopolization of the democratic process by local and regional elites (see also Jaffrelot 2003; and Yadav 2000). They also show a clear tendency for subaltern group rights to be far better served in states where their interests are represented by left-oriented parties holding political power at state level.[19]

In other words, the dynamics within civil and political society are clearly interconnected, and consequently it is safe to argue that "like all binary distinctions, this one is also overdrawn' (Corbridge, Williams, Srivastava and Véron 2005: 256).

We thus find ourselves back at the conceptual challenge I outlined earlier, that of developing a theoretical perspective that makes it possible to analyse power and resistance as relational practices rather than autonomous domains—in other words, to sketch a perspective which prioritizes dialectics above binary oppositions. This is the theme of the next part of this chapter.

Theoretical Orientations 2

In his classic book *Europe and the People Without History,* Eric Wolf sets out a strong critique of the concept of culture in classical anthropology, which sees cultures as systematically integrated wholes, with an inner essence and logic and clear boundaries to other cultures:

> Once we locate the reality of society in historically changing, imperfectly bounded, multiple and branching social alignments [...] the concept of a fixed, unitary, and bounded culture must give way to a sense of fluidity and permeability of cultural sets. (Wolf 1982: 387)

As I argued above, the analysis of power and resistance in Subaltern Studies is characterized by precisely such a concept of culture. Despite the flood of modifications that can be found as asides, both in theoretical postulates and empirical studies it is assumed that dominant and subaltern groups operate within culturally separated and *sui generis* domains, between which an external relation develops in certain circumstances. But the reality that is described, both in Subaltern Studies and analyses of subaltern resistance in today's India, points to the fact that power and resistance are practices which take place within a set of social relationships where cultural and political symbols and horizons of understandings breach the boundaries between dominant and subaltern groups, and are continually constructed, deconstructed and reconstructed precisely through the exercise of power and resistance.

It was just such a conflictual interaction—in other words a struggle over the meaning of political and cultural symbols—which formed part of the main theme in the British Marxist historians' approach to writing history from below. They observed correctly that there are distinct popular cultures, and that these cultures in turn give rise to social movements that challenge the position and legitimacy of dominant social groups. However, these cultures were not postulated as an autonomous unity, separated from the dominant groups' culture, but understood as a result of subaltern appropriation of aspects of the elites' culture and ideology, which were then interpreted and given meaning in ways that reflected their lived experience of, attitude towards and hopes for processes of social change. For example, both Brian Manning (1996, 1999) and Christopher Hill (1991) show how movements of small peasants produced oppositional readings of Bible texts in order to develop an ideology that could legitimate their opposition to the aristocracy and big farmers during the bourgeois revolution in England. In other words, elements which were thoroughly central to the ideological apparatus of the ruling classes were used as weapons against their social dominance. This dynamic is perhaps even more prominent in E.P. Thompson's (1971) interpretation of the 'politics of the people' in eighteenth century England, where the concept of 'moral economy', so central in Subaltern Studies, was first formulated.

I noted above how Subaltern Studies chooses to interpret the concept of subaltern moral economy as a concept based on the small peasants' autonomous, communal ideology. In other words, it is a horizon of understanding which is grounded in entirely different normative principles than those we find in the culture of dominant groups. This was not Thompson's understanding of the concept. In the article 'The Moral Economy of the English Crowd in the Eighteenth Century', Thompson analyses so-called 'food riots'—episodes where subaltern groups challenged millers, bakers and traders who demanded unreasonable prices for flour and bread, and demanded that food prices should observe established conventions. He argues that participants in these riots understood their actions as a legitimate defence of traditional rights and customs which were supported by a consensus within the local community (Thompson 1971: 78). People's grievances were articulated within a cultural framework which prescribed what constituted acceptable practice for millers and bakers.

This consensus was in turn based on 'a consistent traditional view of social norms and obligations, of the proper economic functions of several parties within the community, which, taken together, can be said to constitute the moral economy of the poor' (1971: 79). This understanding of social norms and duties was in turn grounded in a popular interpretation of a state ideology based on a paternalistic tradition—in other words a set of procedures to regulate food sales laid down in legal statutes as well as customary rights, and which English authorities followed in crisis periods right up to the late eighteenth century. Even if the authorities were clear that this model was becoming antiquated in an England that was rapidly moving towards the industrial revolution, it was nonetheless used as a point of reference in situations where people's access to food dramatically worsened: 'In this they were in part the prisoners of the people, who adopted parts of the model as their right and heritage.' (Thompson 1971: 88).

Moral economy, in other words, can be understood as an expression for what can be called 'an articulated consciousness' (T. Sarkar 1985: 161), where subaltern groups make use of elements of dominant groups' ideologies in order to represent their grievances, interests and hopes:

> The customs defended are the people's own [...] But when the people search for legitimations for protest, they often turn back to the paternalist regulations of a more authoritarian society, and select among these the parts most calculated to defend their present interests. (Thompson 1971: 154)

This is also an effective form of resistance, since dominant groups are confronted with the objection that their behaviour breaks with their own moral and normative principles. It is precisely this which gives popular moral economy resonance within the corridors of power, and which makes dominant groups 'prisoners of the people': the oppositional message is mediated through a symbolic code which is at least in part their own, and which they have to relate to if they are to maintain legitimate rule. This dynamic and relational understanding of power and resistance shows how Thompson viewed subaltern groups as part of a social 'field-of-force' where cultural symbols can legitimate both domination and riots—and it was precisely the 'dialectic of culture' that followed from this that was central to his studies of subaltern politics (1978: 151, 150). This perspective highlights the internal relationships between dominant and subaltern groups and the practices through which they seek to exercise and legitimate power and resistance within a historically defined set of social relationships. We are thus moving away from an approach to dominant and subaltern groups grounded in the assumption of autonomous domains and towards an understanding of power and resistance as relational practices.

In order to develop this perspective further, it is useful to return to Gramsci's theories of hegemony, popular consciousness and resistance. My argument here is that Subaltern Studies, like many orthodox Marxists, read Gramsci's theory of hegemony as a concept that describes such an all-encompassing form of cultural power that subaltern consciousness and horizons of understanding are exclusively defined by the dominant groups' culture and ideology.[20] One of the project's most central contributors, David Arnold, for example, asserts that Gramsci sought to use his concept of hegemony to explain dominant groups' total political, cultural and ideological power over the masses, and that he tends to exaggerate the strength of hegemony (Arnold 1984). Similar arguments can also be found in Ranajit Guha (1989). In my view this is a mistaken reading of Gramsci—both in terms of what form of power hegemony actually constitutes, and in terms of his perspective on subaltern groups' consciousness and oppositional practice.

Gramsci defined hegemony as the adherence of social majorities to dominant groups' organization and development of society (1998: 12, 181). The development of society reflects the interests of dominant groups, but these interests appear as general and universal ones. This does not mean that we are dealing with a fixed, monolithic state of affairs. Hegemony is the result of a complex, conflictual process where groups which seek to achieve a dominant position combine the interests of different social groups within a 'historical bloc' that forms the basis for the exercise of power (Roseberry 1994: 357–360; Crehan 2002: 92–93; and O'Hanlon 2002: 180). This process begins with the formation of ties between members of specific professional and status groups—Gramsci calls this the economic-corporative level—and is further developed by the coming together of whole social groups as collective actors. He describes the further development and final result of this process thus:

> A third moment is that in which one becomes aware that one's own corporate interests, in their present and future development, transcend the corporate limits of the purely economic class, and can and must become the interests of other subordinate groups too [...] it is the phase in which previously germinated ideologies become 'party', come into confrontation and conflict, until one of them, or at least a single combination of them, tends to prevail, to gain the upper hand, to propagate itself throughout society—bringing about not only a unison of economic and political aims, but also intellectual and moral unity, posing all the questions around which the struggle rages not on a corporate level but on a 'universal' plane, and thus creating the hegemony of a fundamental social group over a series of subordinate groups [...] In other words, the dominant group is co-ordinated concretely with the general interests of the subordinate groups, and the life of the State is conceived of as a continuous process of formation and superseding of unstable equilibria [...] between the fundamental group and those of the

> subordinate groups—equilibria in which the interests of the dominant group prevail, but only up to a certain point, i.e. stopping short of narrowly corporate economic interest. (Gramsci 1998: 181-182)

As Roseberry (1994: 359-360) points out, this is a process which not only involves building bridges between dominant groups whose shared interests cannot necessarily be taken for granted, but also a process where dominant groups must win the adherence of subaltern groups. This entails a confrontation in which dominant groups must take a position on and concede some subaltern demands and interests in order to be able to appear as representatives of general and universal interests. Subalterns, in other words, are not passive in their adherence to the hegemony of dominant groups, and hegemony must thus be understood as an incomplete process which must be constantly 'renewed, recreated, defended, and modified' (Williams 1977: 112), rather than a permanent and already-achieved state of affairs.

The tension between adhering to this hegemony and challenging it from below is tied up with Gramsci's understanding of the contradictory nature of subaltern consciousness. The first thing we should note is that Gramsci does not see subaltern groups as 'inhabitants' of an autonomous social and political domain, but as part of a social field of force where they exist in relation to dominant groups:

> The history of subaltern social groups is necessarily fragmented and episodic. There undoubtedly does exist a tendency to (at least provisional stages of) unification in the historical activity of these groups, but this tendency is continually interrupted by the activity of ruling groups

> [...] Subaltern groups are always subject to the activity of ruling groups, even when they rebel and rise up: only 'permanent' victory breaks their subordination, and that not immediately. (Gramsci 1998: 55)

What Gramsci asserts here is of course that subalterns' lifeworlds, both in everyday and extraordinary situations—such as around resistance and insurgency—are moved, shaped and formed by dominant groups and their economic, social, political and cultural practices. This in turn is expressed in subaltern groups' consciousness. Gramsci designated this form of consciousness as 'common sense' and emphasized its contradictory character: on the one side, this consciousness is formed by subaltern groups' adoption of dominant groups' culture and ideologies, and this aspect of their consciousness underlies their adherence to the existing social order. On the other side, they also possess horizons of understanding which stand in opposition to hegemonic ideologies, which reflect their own interests as subaltern groups, and which appear in those moments when they resist dominant groups (Gramsci 1998: 333). Gramsci described the oppositional aspect of the consciousness of the dominated as 'good sense'—the 'healthy nucleus' within 'common sense' (1998: 328)—and he described its meaning thus:

> It signifies that the social group in question may indeed have its own conception of the world, even if only embryonic; a conception which manifests itself in action, but occassionally and in flashes—when, that is, the group is acting as an organic totality. (Gramsci 1998: 327)

It is precisely these contradictions within subaltern groups' consciousness which constitute the limits of hegemony, and which form the underlying reason why it must be constantly defended and renewed in response to challenges from below.

For Gramsci, this contradictory consciousness was not a permanent state of affairs but a form of consciousness with a potential for development (1998: 333). Subaltern groups, according to Gramsci, were able to develop a more critical understanding of a given social order, of their position within the structures of this order, and of how this order could be changed by political action. It was precisely through such an active process—the political struggle for social change—that subaltern groups would be able to break away from hegemonic ideologies and dominant groups' ideological legitimation of the order of things. This struggle, however, does not take place as a mobilization within an autonomous domain. It is a matter of a gradual development of political practices in relation to dominant groups and their institutions, practices and symbols within a social field of force.

It was precisely this that underlay Gramsci's formulation of a programme for the study of the subaltern classes in the *Prison Notebooks* (1998: 52). As Green (2002) notes, this is not only a historiographical methodology, but also a schematic presentation of the learning processes which subaltern groups go through in developing their oppositional practices in a conflictual interaction with dominant groups. Ranajit Guha did indeed flirt, in the foreword to the series' first volume, with precisely this formulation of a programme to study subaltern politics, but dismissed the possibility of achieving such a massive task (1982: vii).

If we nonetheless make the attempt, I argue that we will be able to approach a precise analysis of how subaltern politics consists of a set of more or less oppositional practices which are developed in relation to the exercise of power by dominant groups, and which constantly set limits to this exercise of power. We will also recognize that subaltern autonomy is a result of this learning process rather than an already-existing domain, a product of successful political mobilization rather than the starting point for oppositional movements, as it is formulated in Subaltern Studies and studies of new social movements inspired by the idea that subaltern politics is developed within an autonomous domain.

Such a programme would take as a theoretical starting-point that dominant and subaltern groups exist in relation to one another within a social field of force. Within this field of force, there is a cultural dialectic as a result of the fact that social groups with conflicting interests are struggling over the interpretation of cultural symbols and horizons of understanding in their attempt to exercise and legitimate power and resistance. If this perspective is used in the study of India's independence movement or the analysis of new social movements and new forms of oppositional politics among subaltern groups, parallel dynamics will be encountered.

Firstly: the social field of force, and relations between dominant and subaltern groups in these fields, will change rapidly—in one case as a result of India's imbrication in the political economy of colonialism, in the other as a result of nearly two decades of market-oriented reforms and an ever-closer imbrication in a global, neoliberal economic order. Secondly: as a result of these processes of change, subaltern groups will be exposed to various forms of resource dispossession—in one case typically related to the results of the colonial authorities' agricultural regime and in the other typically related to state developmental projects or the introduction of neoliberal strategies of accumulation.

At the same time, their ties of loyalty to dominant groups and their political institutions—be they feudal landowners and their ideologies or national political parties and their vote bank machines—are eroding.

Thirdly: as a challenge to these processes of change and their social consequences, we will find that subaltern groups seek to articulate oppositional practices and discourses, and that these discourses and practices are often marked by their basis in an appropriation, reinterpretation and adaptation of dominant groups' discourses and practices to subaltern needs—whether it is a question of feudal ideologies, national independence projects, modern development ideologies or the state's political and administrative practices. The question of how far this process will lead towards an autonomous position for subaltern groups will remain an open question and, as Gramsci formulated it (1998: 55), can only be resolved once a historical cycle of struggles has come to an end—whether in the form of victory, defeat or a more or less unstable compromise between the conflicting parties.

By way of conclusion, I want to note that the questions which have been raised in this chapter in relation to our understanding of power and resistance in the relationship between dominant and subaltern groups are not only to be understood as a theoretical and analytical matter. They are, fundamentally, highly significant political questions. Gramsci describes activists' practice as follows:

> The active politician is a creator and an initiator; but he neither creates from nothing nor does he move in the turbid void of his own desires and dreams. He bases himself on effective reality [...] If one applies one's will to the creation of a new equilibrium among the forces which really exist and are operative [...] one still moves

> on the terrain of effective reality, but does so in order to dominate and transcend it (or to contribute to this). (Gramsci 1998: 172)

The founders of Subaltern Studies were very concerned that their historiographical practice should contribute to the development of popular resistance in India—and this is an ambition shared by many of those researching today's social movements. I want to assert that this ambition will be better served by developing a perspective that sees power and resistance as relational practices, and which understands subaltern politics as a process which arises and develops through the appropriation and reinterpretation of dominant ideologies and active use of existing political institutions and practices. Through such a perspective, in my view, we can come closer to the actual reality which subaltern groups operate in relation to when they develop their oppositional projects. And by doing this, we can open up a discussion on the possible limitations of such political practices—a discussion which in turn can play a role in the further development of oppositional practices capable of breaking with existing, institutionalized power relations and their ideological legitimation.

Notes

1 Alongside Ranajit Guha, Partha Chatterjee, Gyan Pandey, Sumit Sarkar, David Hardiman, David Arnold, Shahid Amin, Dipesh Chakrabarty and Gayatri Chakravorty Spivak have been among the most central contributors to *Subaltern Studies*, of which 11 volumes have been published to date.

2 Guha (1982) indicates his ambiguity around the proletariat's role in the Indian independence struggle by arguing that this class was never sufficiently mature to establish leadership over and give shape to Indian nationalism. Dipesh Chakrabarty (1983, 1984, 1989) analyses the industrial working class as a subaltern group and argues that Indian workers were marked by a traditional consciouness, grounded in the culture they brought from the village, rather than by a modern consciousness of class interests and class struggle. This perspective has in turn been sharply criticized by, among

others, Rajnarayan Chandavarkar (1994), Subho Basu (2004) and Vinay Bahl (1995).

3 The series' first five volumes also covered other themes, such as small peasants' militant response to famine, religious communalism, subalterns' relationship to laws on alcohol, as well as individual attempts to study more everyday forms of resistance among subaltern groups.

4 It should also be noted that the contributors to *Subaltern Studies* have published a range of monograph elaborating on the studies they published in article form in the series. Among these we can mention Ranajit Guha's (1983a) study of the elementary structures of peasant insurgency, Pandey's (1978) study of the Congress movement's growth in Uttar Pradesh, Hardiman's (1987a) study of the Devi movement among Adivasis in Gujarat, Partha Chatterjee's (1986) critique of Indian nationalism and nation-building and Sumit Sarkar's (1983) study of the role of radical social movements in the Indian independence struggle from 1885 to 1947.

5 E.P. Thompson, who was elected president of the Indian History Congress in the late 1970s, was perhaps particularly important in this respect; see Chandavarkar (2000) and Sarkar (2000) for commentaries.

6 But as David Ludden (2003: 15) notes, Guha used the *Concise Oxford Dictionary* rather than Gramsci's *Prison Notebooks* to define 'subaltern' in the first volume of *Subaltern Studies*. This hints at the series' unresolved and unclear relationship to Gramsci's theories on hegemony and resistance.

7 The Naxalite movement is still alive and kicking, controlling an area referred to as the Red Corridor, which stretches throughout extensive rural areas in eastern and southeastern India (see Shah 2011, 2014; Sundar 2012; Mukherji 2012).

8 The first three volumes of *Subaltern Studies* were mainly read and debated by an Indian public (Ludden 2003).

9 This turn was signalled by Gayatri Chakravorty Spivak's (1985, 1988) commentaries on and participation in the collective's work, as well as by Edward Said's foreword to the *Selected Subaltern Studies* edited collection, which introduced an American audience to the series in 1988.

10 See Ludden (2003); see also Sivaramakrishnan (2002) and Cooper (2002). A crucial contribution here is Ranajit Guha's (1989) essay 'Dominance Without Hegemony', published in the series' seventh volume. This turn also gave birth to a vital debate on postcolonial historiography, with contributions from Rosalind O'Hanlon and David Washbrook (1992), Gyan Prakash (1990, 1992a, 1992b, 1994), Dipesh Chakrabarty (1995) and Sumit Sarkar (1994, 2002).

11 This is not in itself a particularly original perspective, but a continuous theme in the debate on Subaltern Studies, and I will actively draw on a rich spectrum of commentaries, from the earliest responses by Indian academics on. See Chopra (1982) and Alam (2002); as well as more recent contributions such as O'Hanlon (2002); Sivaramakrishnan (2002); and Cooper (2002).

12 This is obviously a very general description of the actual 'content' of subaltern groups' politics and political consciousness. It should therefore be

noted that Guha goes into far more detail in his important book *Elementary Aspects of Peasant Insurgency in Colonial India* (1983a), where he presents an analysis of the collective mentalities that gave shape and meaning to peasant insurgency in colonial India. For reasons of space, I will not go into this exposition in this chapter.

13 This observation is a central theme in Partha Chatterjee's (1986, 1993) theories on India's 'passive revolution'. See also Guha 1989 and Kaviraj (1997).

14 James Scott (1976) developed this concept further in his study of peasant insurgencies in Southeast Asia, but it is above all Thompson's use of the concept which is employed and discussed in Subaltern Studies, with the exception of David Arnold (1982), who criticizes Scott for lacking a class perspective in his use of the concept.

15 In this connection see also Arnold (1982); Sarkar, T. (1985); and Hardiman (1987b).

16 This point is also recognized by Sumit Sarkar (1984) in his contribution to the third volume of *Subaltern Studies*. See also Cooper (2002: 272).

17 This perspective is typically also influenced by Arturo Escobar's (1995) theory that new social movements in the global South reject the modern discourse of development in its entirety.

18 Chatterjee sees these categories as part of the apparatus constructed by the modern state in order to create what Foucault called 'governmentality'.

19 This observation is also confirmed at a district level by Stuart Corbridge, Glyn Williams, Manoj Srivastava and René Véron (2005) in their study of poor groups' relationship to the state in eastern India.

20 See Thompson (1971: 164) for a critique of this perspective. See also Williams (1977: 108–114).

2

For a Historical Sociology of State-Society Relations in the Study of Subaltern Politics

This chapter presents a critical discussion of the theoretical frameworks through which state-society relations have been conceptualized in the study of subaltern resistance in colonial and postcolonial India. In developing this discussion, I will argue for the necessity of developing a historical sociology of state formation grounded in Marxian theory in order to be adequately equipped to analyse the ways in which subaltern resistance articulates with state power and the institutions, discourses and technologies of rule through which this power is effectuated.

The first part of the chapter presents a critical assessment of the Subaltern Studies project's conceptualization of the relationship between the state and subaltern groups in colonial and postcolonial India. Engaging with the work of Ranajit Guha, Partha Chatterjee, and Sudipta Kaviraj, I call attention to the problems arising from a persistently bifurcated view of state power and subaltern resistance. This perspective, I argue, fails to appreciate how subaltern groups appropriate the institutions, discourses, and governmental technologies of the state when they engage in collective resistance.

I then consider an alternative to this perspective that has recently come to the fore, namely ethnographic studies of everyday forms of state-society relations and encounters that draw on Foucault's notion of governmentality. Focusing on the work of Akhil Gupta and Aradhana Sharma, I argue that these perspectives have been of great importance in crafting a more relational conception of the multifarious ways in which subaltern groups in India conceive of and engage with the state. However, due to their commitment to a decentred and dispersed understanding of power, these perspectives fail to engage sufficiently with how historically determinate relations of class power tend to both enable *and* constrain the pursuit of subaltern politics in and through the state.

In the third and final section, I outline an alternative approach to the study of state-society relations which is grounded in Gramsci's conceptions of sub-alternity, hegemony, and state formation. The objective of this exercise is to construct a foundation for a historical-sociological approach to the study of subaltern politics that enables us to decipher the dialectics of enablement and constraint that emerge at the point of convergence between the contemporary micro-dynamics of everyday state-society relations and the macro-structural *longue durée* of state formation.

State-Society Relations in the Subaltern Studies Project

As I pointed out in chapter 1, the Subaltern Studies project took its point of departure from Ranajit Guha's founding statement in the essay 'On Some Aspects of the Historiography of Colonial India', in which he argued for a conceptualization of the politics of subaltern groups as an 'autonomous domain' that 'neither originated from elite politics, nor did its existence depend on the latter' (Guha 1982: 4).

This conception of subaltern politics as an autonomous domain had significant implications for how state-society relations were conceived of by key participants in the Subaltern Studies project. A close reading of the relevant texts reveals the contours of a conceptual narrative that runs as follows: the precolonial state was a very distant entity for most subaltern groups, who seem to have inhabited something akin to James Scott's (2010) 'non-state spaces'. Despite intentions and attempts to the contrary, the marginality of the state in relation to the lifeworlds of India's subaltern minorities was reproduced under colonialism. And the postcolonial state has at best been only partially successful in overcoming this schism, which in effect means that it remains largely alien and irrelevant to the articulation and pursuit of subaltern politics.

Precolonial and Colonial State-Society Relations in the Subaltern Studies Project

As I showed above, Partha Chatterjee's (1982, 1983a) early contributions to the Subaltern Studies project focused on how different 'modes of power' structure and animate particular social formations. Chatterjee argues that precolonial peasant societies have their basis in a 'communal mode of power', which binds together the peasantry in a community where 'the collective is always prior to the individual parts and its authority larger than the mere sum of its parts' (Chatterjee 1982: 12). Peasant consciousness, in turn, is one in which 'the state is always distant'—it remains 'an entity which is not organic or integral to the familiar sphere of everyday social activity' (ibid.: 31–32).

Thus, when 'peasant-communal politics' engages with the state—and the state and its functionaries are perennial targets of peasant discontent—'it is always the concept of the community as a whole, a form of authority incapable of being broken down into its constituent parts, which shapes and directs peasant politics *vis-à-vis* the state' (ibid.: 34-35; see also Chatterjee 1983a). Sudipta Kaviraj has developed a similar perspective in which he argues that the precolonial state was 'a distant, formally all-encompassing empire' that commanded ceremonial deference from its subjects, but had little actual capacity for intervention in their communities, lifeworlds and livelihoods (Kaviraj 2010a: 12). In this sense, the precolonial state was situated at the centre of 'a circle of circles of caste and regional communities' in which monarchical rulers were afforded 'deep obeisance at the cost of a certain marginality' (Kaviraj 2012b: 53).

Now, the advent of colonial rule brought in its tow a serious commitment to overcome this marginality. In the political realm, this revolved around a partial introduction of modernist political discourse, centred on 'the idea of the state as an impersonal regime of relations, the idea of an individual subject ... the equality of rights or rightlessness ... and, finally, a state which ... pretended to represent the collective interest of society, and whose legitimate interference in society was morally immune' (Kaviraj 2010a: 12).[1] Education served as a means to induct a small Indian elite into the running of the new politico-administrative apparatus and more generally into the incipient public sphere that—despite its exclusions and inequalities—was constituted by and through the colonial project. In other words, the imperial polity 'provided a discursive space on which nationalist ideas could eventually be framed' (Kaviraj 2012b: 50) by turning 'the political point of this discourse against colonial authority itself' (ibid.: 20).

For Chatterjee, of course, the formation of the Indian national state was a paradigmatic case of 'passive revolution' in which a structurally weak but aspiring bourgeoisie sought to build 'the largest possible nationalist alliance ... against the political rule of the colonial power' (ibid.: 48). But this also entailed confronting the 'fundamental cultural problem' (Chatterjee 1986: 48) of overcoming the parochial traditionalism of the peasant's world view.

In *Nationalist Thought in the Colonial World*, Chatterjee traces the career of this problem through the sequential development of Indian nationalist ideology across three phases—the moments of departure, manoeuvre, and arrival respectively—as these were embodied in the thought of three leading nationalists: Bankimchandra Chattopadhyay, Mahatma Gandhi, and Jawaharlal Nehru (Chatterjee 1986). The key point for Chatterjee is that throughout these three moments the peasantry and its politics remained marginalized. This marginalization was ultimately institutionalized when Indian nationalism became 'a *state ideology*' (ibid.: 132) in and through the Nehruvian nation-building project, in which 'the life of the nation' was subsumed under 'the life of the state' (ibid.: 161).

Similarly to Chatterjee, Kaviraj sees anticolonial nationalism as a project which germinated among the narrow Indian elite that was incorporated into the colonial state machinery, and which then turned the precepts of liberal political discourse against the colonial rulers: 'Indian nationalism, at least the form in which it came to be enshrined in the Congress, was primarily a product of this discourse, a complex of dissatisfactions worked out by the modernist-rationalistic elite' (ibid.: 2010). The postcolonial state that eventually emerged as a result of anticolonial mobilization consequently also reproduced many of the exclusions that had been constitutive of the colonial state. Indeed, according to Kaviraj (ibid.: 23), the mobilizing strategies of the Indian freedom movement established an elite-subaltern relation that after 1947 'would be written as the state-society relation'.

Finally, it is worth taking note of Guha's own formulation of this argument in the long essay 'Dominance Without Hegemony' (Guha 1989). Guha's point of departure in the argument is that in colonial India 'power simply stood for a series of inequalities between the rulers and the ruled as well as between classes, strata and individuals among the latter' (ibid.: 229).[2] Guha attributes these unequal relationships and power differentials to a specific structuring of dominance and subordination under the Raj. Hegemony, Guha argues, is a form of dominance in which persuasion outweighs coercion. However, the colonial state 'failed to generate a hegemonic ruling culture' (Guha 1998: 64). Ultimately, the reason for this failure is located in the essentially alien and imposed character of the colonial state: 'The colonial state in India did not originate from the activity of Indian society itself ... As an *absolute externality*, it was *structured like a despotism* with no mediating depths, no space provided for a transaction between the will of the rulers and that of the ruled' (Guha 1989: 274-275). Under these conditions, British rule over Asian subjects came to rely 'more on force than consent' (ibid.: 281)—that is, 'dominance without hegemony' (ibid.: 282).

The fundamental problem with the underlying narrative in these accounts lies in its postulation of a profound disjuncture between subaltern groups and precolonial and colonial forms of state. This is, quite simply, a claim that fails to measure up to the historical evidence. Precolonial peasant protest—such as the *dhandak* in the Tehri-Garwal

Himalayas (Guha 1985, 1999)—was clearly animated by a culture of resistance that operated through an oppositional appropriation of the ideology of kingship that underpinned precolonial states. Now, obviously, the 'infrastructural power' (Mann 1984) of precolonial states was constrained by 'the political economy of appropriation' (Haldon 1993) that undergirded tributary modes of production (see also Berktay 1991 and Banaji 2010). Nevertheless, the fact that cultures of resistance such as the *dhandak* existed suggests that it is highly problematic to construe the peasant community and the state as independent and opposing entities which only enter into an external relation with each other in and through conflictual clashes.

Similar problems attach to claims about the colonial state and subaltern resistance during the Raj. Contrary to the claim that peasant communities simply opposed the state as an externality, a recent study of Adivasi resistance in colonial Chota Nagpur has shown that the tribal peasantry in this region would petition the state all the way from the local level to London, deploying a rhetoric that 'admirably mimics the official discourse of colonial primitivism' (Chandra 2013a: 154). Even when they made politico-theological claims to sovereignty, the demand was for 'quasi-national autonomy under British colonial overlordship' (ibid.: 157). Moreover, as Kaushik Ghosh (2006: 525) points out, the fact that the colonial state came to recognize Adivasi land rights through protective legislation cannot be understood as anything other than 'a cumulative effect of massive and persistent tribal revolts against the colonial system of eighteenth and nineteenth century India and Jharkhand.'

In other words, actual historical dynamics seem to compel us to develop a far more fine-grained analytic of relations between the precolonial and colonial states and subaltern groups than what is allowed for by a formulation like 'dominance without hegemony'.

Postcolonial State-Society Relations in and beyond the Subaltern Studies Project

Dominance without hegemony during the Raj was, according to Ranajit Guha (1989: 307), reproduced by its 'successor regime'—the postcolonial Indian state. While this claim is not developed in any depth in Guha's own work, it has been a central theme in the critiques of the Indian nation-state issued by Kaviraj and Chatterjee.

According to Sudipta Kaviraj, the Nehruvian nation-building project was by no means grounded in the political vocabulary of the popular classes. Rather, it was anchored in ideals that were intelligible and relevant only to the modernizing elite that had taken over the reins of power from the British. Therefore, the commanding heights of the state came to be dominated by an elite that 'did not try to create or re-constitute popular common sense around the political world, taking the new conceptual vocabulary of rights, institutions, and impersonal power into the vernacular discourse of rural or small-town Indian society' (Kaviraj 2010: 29).

As the Indian state expanded, this created a bifurcation between the 'upper' and 'lower' discourses of the state: 'The new elite could not create its own hegemony, or create a dialogic relation with the subaltern classes' (Kaviraj 2010: 81). The postcolonial state came to rely on 'a vast lower-order population'—those who did not 'inhabit the modernist discourse'—in recruiting its personnel and implementing its policies (ibid.: 26, 30). This means that, at the point of implementation, major government policies originally infused with elite conceptions of governance and development have been 'reinterpreted beyond recognition' (ibid.: 30). Thus, despite the fact that the state 'in its sordid everyday structures' has become more familiar to India's subaltern groups, a deep-seated 'problem of intelligibility of the political institutions of the state remains at the heart of the Indian democratic system' (ibid.: 246).

The central arguments presented in Chatterjee's second treatise on Indian nationalism—*The Nation and its Fragments*—tap a similar vein. The postcolonial nation state, he argues, has constructed its self-definition 'from the ideology of the modern, liberal-democratic state' and as a result of this, 'autonomous forms of imagination of the community were, and continue to be, overwhelmed and swamped by the history of the postcolonial state.' (Chatterjee 1993: 10-11).

It is nevertheless possible to detect a slight change in the tenor of his argument—a change that in many ways mirrors the claims put forward by Kaviraj—in that he stresses a certain tenuous rapprochement between elite and subaltern politics in relation to the postcolonial state. The fact that both communalism and populism have become increasingly salient phenomena within the context of India's liberal constitutional order is interpreted as an indication of a two-pronged change: on the one hand, Indian elites have come to recognize that their political fortunes depend to a large extent on electoral support from subaltern groups, and that this can only be achieved with these groups through demotic idioms and imaginaries; on the other hand, the subaltern domain of politics 'has increasingly become familiar with, and even adapted itself to, the institutional realms of the elite domain' (ibid.: 13).

Still, it is all too clear that Chatterjee's analytical optic still rests upon the assumption that there exist two separate political domains—one defined by 'the hegemonic project of nationalist modernity' and the other by 'the numerous fragmented resistances to that project' (ibid.: 13; see also 218-19). In his more recent work, Chatterjee has suggested that—as a result of the deepening reach of the developmental state under electoral democracy' (Chatterjee 2008: 54)—subaltern groups have become more familiar with the governmental technologies of the state. However, as many critics have noted—for example Sundar (2011) and Sinha (2012)—his distinction between 'civil society' as a sphere of elite politics and 'political society' as a sphere of subaltern politics fails to capture how actually-existing subaltern politics is often crafted around oppositional claims for citizenship (see also Agarwala 2013; Subramanian 2009; Baviskar and Sundar 2008; Chandra 2013b; Nilsen 2012a; Chopra, Williams, and Vira 2011).

It is clearly necessary to develop a fine-grained understanding of the mutual imbrication of subaltern politics and the institutions, discourses, and technologies of rule of the state. In the next section of this chapter, I therefore move on to discuss a body of scholarship that seeks to make sense of this mutual imbrication by employing Foucauldian concepts in the ethnographic study of state-society relations.

Foucauldian Studies of State-Society Relations in India

Foucauldian ethnographies of state-society relations in India have mushroomed in recent years through the work of scholars as diverse as Akhil Gupta (1995, 1998, 2001, 2012), Aradhana Sharma (2008; see also Gupta and

Sharma 2006a/b), Chris Fuller and John Harriss (2001); Stuart Corbridge, Glyn Williams, Manoj Srivastava and René Véron (2005), and Philippa Williams, Bhaskar Vira and Deepta Chopra (2011). In the following, I will focus predominantly on the work of Akhil Gupta and Aradhana Sharma, as they are arguably the ones who have developed this perspective in the richest and most stimulating manner since the mid-1990s.[3]

Akhil Gupta on Governmentality and Subaltern Politics in Rural India

In a landmark article on the discursive construction of the state, Akhil Gupta (1995: 375) argues that 'the state has become implicated in the minute texture of everyday life' in contemporary India. However, in contrast to Kaviraj's notion of upper-order and lower-order discourses about the state, Gupta insists on the importance of not conceiving of the local state as a coherent spatial unit that encapsulates its own reality. Whereas the *tehsil* (sub-district) is obviously the arena where the vast majority of Indians come into contact with the state and where their imaginaries of the state are forged, Gupta argues for the need to acknowledge that the local state is itself criss-crossed by translocal processes, discourses and practices that in turn modify subaltern imaginaries of the state (ibid.: 377).

Using the example of corruption, Gupta (1995: 389) argues that 'the imagined state' crystallizes at the confluence of, on the one hand, the experience of encounters with corruption in the practices of the local bureaucracy, and, on the other hand, the discourse of corruption as it is articulated in public culture. Local experiences with corruption are endemic, but also varied; in Gupta's account they range from cases where villagers fail to master the art of giving a bribe, thereby finding themselves under the thumb of local revenue officials, via the recalcitrant low-caste farmer who is at least partially successful in challenging corruption in a government housing programme, to the militant farmers of the Bharatiya Kisan Union, who regularly cajole local officials into delivering state development schemes.

What cuts across these experiences and encounters, however, is that the state is perceived as being embedded in and entwined with local relations of power (Gupta 1995: 384). Practical experiences of corruption and the awareness that this generates about how the state is implicated in local power relations in turn mesh with the discourse of corruption that circulates in public culture—in particular, through the vernacular press. This discourse, Gupta argues, constructs an opposition between an exploitative state and an exploited people, and in doing so it appeals to the notion of citizenship that was so central to the establishment of the postcolonial state. The state is therefore constructed discursively as an entity that is accountable to the people: 'The discourse of corruption, by marking those actions that constitute an infringement of such rights, thus acts to represent the rights of citizens to themselves ... The discourse of corruption ... plays this dual role of enabling people to construct the state symbolically and to define themselves as citizens' (ibid.: 389).

Gupta draws out a series of implications for the study of the state and state-society relations from this argument. He maintains that the state must be conceptualized in a more disaggregated and less bounded way than has been the case hitherto—that is, it is necessary to conceive of the state as a space constituted at the intersection of local, regional, national and global political flows. In political terms, this also means that absolute distinctions between collaboration and resistance are unsatisfactory. Strategically, Gupta argues, it is important to exploit the contradictions in the workings of state institutions, discourses, and governmental technologies. These 'fissures and ruptures' enable subaltern groups 'to create possibilities for political action and activism' (ibid.: 394).[4]

This perspective is developed further and takes on a more explicitly Foucauldian character in Gupta's (2001) analysis of the Integrated Child Development Services (ICDS) programme in Uttar Pradesh. According to Gupta, the ICDS is best conceptualized via Foucault's notion of governmentality—that is, a form of power that is exercised through the workings of dispersed techniques of government that seek to improve the welfare of a population in various ways.[5] Given its preoccupation with 'the size and quality of the population' and its reliance on 'techniques of regulation, enumeration, and accountability', the ICDS has driven a vast expansion of the scope and reach of the state into the lives of poor people in the Indian countryside, and in particular into the lives of lower caste women and their children (ibid.: 74).

However, Gupta (2001: 66) is keen to emphasize that the implementation of the ICDS did not merely create new subjects—it also created 'new kinds of resistances'. Each node in the ICDS chain of command was also a site where these resistances played themselves out: in the face of *anganwadi* workers who tried to collect a variety of statistics and data from and about them, poor rural women would refuse these workers access to their homes and refuse to provide certain kinds of information; in the face of bureaucrats who defined them as "volunteers", the women *anganwadi* workers challenged this lowly status and defined themselves as "teachers" (ibid.: 74-92).

Thus, whereas the contemporary Indian state is clearly involved in a concerted effort to 'alter, regulate, monitor, measure, record, and reward the conduct of politically disempowered groups of lower-caste women and children' so as to manage the size and quality of the population, it is also and conversely true that 'the conduct of government itself' changes as a result of the interaction that goes on in and through state-society relations, as subaltern groups imbue 'the state with their own agendas, interpretations, and actions' (ibid.: 92).[6]

Aradhana Sharma on Neoliberal Empowerment and Subaltern Assertion

Aradhana Sharma (2008) develops the Foucauldian approach to the understanding of state-society relations in contemporary India with reference to the intersection between NGO activism and official policy strategies for women's empowerment.

Sharma investigates the workings of the *Mahila Samakhya* (MS), the Indian government's flagship programme for women's empowerment in Uttar Pradesh. Now, on the part of the state, MS represents a turn away from a developmentalist form of governmentality centred on welfare and towards a neoliberal form of governmentality centred on efforts 'to empower marginalized subjects to care for themselves' (Sharma, 2008: 69). A common criticism of NGO and activist participation in programmes such as these is that it ultimately leads to their co-optation and depoliticization. However, according to Sharma, this view is too one-sided: despite their neoliberal tinge, she maintains, programmes like MS 'do not depoliticize struggle as much as they open up new vistas and forms of political action' (ibid.: 64).[7]

In Sharma's study, this is brought out most clearly when she hones in on how MS workers mobilized around issues that involved the state in some way, and that necessitated confrontation and claims-making. Formally speaking, MS workers were government employees, and state officials would actively use this fact as a way of preventing the MS programme from becoming too activist in its orientations. Therefore, MS workers had to find ways to circumvent strictures imposed on them as a result of being government staff. Sharma (2008: 77) details how MS workers 'worked around the state's disciplinary strategies' (ibid.: 77) to achieve empowerment. Crucially, this entailed the use of bureaucratic proceduralism—both to shield themselves from punitive responses from the state and to be able to pursue claims and struggles on behalf of subaltern women (ibid.: 76-9).

Sharma argues that whereas empowerment programmes such as MS clearly governmentalize women's everyday lives and subject them to the disciplinary reach of the state, they also generate knowledge, skills and aptitudes that enable assertion: '... encountering officials, gaining information about how bureaucracies work, and learning statist methods can also be seen as enabling subaltern women to mobilize and demand accountability and entitlements from state agencies' (Sharma, 2008: 75). These reflections echo Gupta's concern with the necessity of using the contradictions, cracks, and fissures in the workings of policies and programmes to advance the concerns of subaltern groups, and focus attention on what might be called the 'unintended consequences' of neoliberal governmentality.

Neoliberal policies, then, may well be geared towards redirecting poor people's gaze from the state to 'themselves, their communities and other civil society bodies', but an unintended consequence of their workings is to generate assertive and oppositional practices that target the agencies of the state: '... this is a politics of citizenship centred on demanding resources as rights from government bodies' (Sharma 2009: xxii). What ultimately emerged from these processes was a discourse of 'justice, rights and citizenship, albeit not one limited to the bourgeois precepts of the individual rights-bearing citizen' (ibid.: 143). Rather, the subaltern communities that Sharma focuses on developed a 'culturally coded, collectively informed' conception of citizenship that effectively denaturalized 'the legalistic discourse on citizenship that writes out questions of class, caste and gender inequality and appears to treat all citizens as formally equal' (ibid.: 144).

Foucauldian Ethnographies: Towards a Critique

Foucauldian ethnographies have situated subaltern politics in contemporary India in 'relational spaces of connection and articulation' (Moore 1998: 347) and in doing so they have been of singular importance in terms of moving beyond the impasses that I discussed in the first part of this chapter. Moreover, by highlighting how the state—rather than being a behemoth defined by 'verticality' and 'encompassment' (Ferguson and Gupta 2002)—is 'a multi-layered and conflictual ensemble' (Gupta and Sharma 2006a: 291), these ethnographies are politically enabling as they make it possible to pursue a debate about how activism can best exploit the schisms that might exist between different scales and regions of the state.

However, despite these significant virtues, I nevertheless believe that this approach to the study of state-society relations and subaltern politics suffers from a theoretical elision that ultimately also limits its political fruitfulness. This elision arises from its theoretical grounding in the analytics of state power that Foucault developed in his lectures on biopolitics and governmentality at the Collège de France (see especially Foucault 2007, 2008). The key problem with this shift is that it leaves us ill-equipped to address the crucial dialectic between what Bob Jessop (1982: 224) has referred to as 'conjunctural possibilities' and 'structural constraints' in subaltern encounters with state power.

The basic problem is this: the argument that 'the state' is not an entity endowed with a clearly demarcated and bounded unity, positioned over and above society, also entails that 'the political power that is pre-eminently ascribed to the state' (Poulantzas 1978: 147) comes to function as a modality in and through which the ability of dominant social groups to control social relations is institutionalized and consolidated. This is perhaps most clearly shown in those historical conjunctures when the exercise of state power achieves a certain unity across dispersed sites as hegemonic groups are faced with concerted challenges from below. However, it is equally visible in the fact that the state is structured in such a way that dominant groups are better able to pursue collective projects in and through the state (Jessop 1990: 250).

If we return to the empirical terrain in question—the postcolonial Indian polity—we find examples of the former in state-orchestrated mobilizations of organized violence in various forms in response to the collective action of subaltern groups,[8] as well as in Indira Gandhi's declaration of a state of emergency in 1975. In a less dramatic but no less significant manner, extensive networks of middlemen, advisers, contractors and criminals are capable of hollowing out the actual state apparatus, depleting its funds, and running it according to their own interests (Harriss-White 2003). Similarly, dominant farming communities often combine their extensive networks of contacts and influence with their substantial purchasing power in the informal market for government jobs in order to colonize the state apparatus and put it to use as a modality for the systematic reproduction of class advantage (Jeffrey 2001; see also Jeffrey and Lerche 2001). These are aspects of the workings of state power that Foucauldian ethnographies of the state cannot adequately grasp. Indeed, in the work of Gupta and Sharma there is no systematic discussion of how class power moulds the institutional modalities of the state and how this structuring in turn reproduces the hegemony of dominant groups.[9]

These elisions arguably echo lacunae in Foucault's theorization of power relations and the state that persisted throughout the different phases of his work. As much as Foucault's early work examined 'sites of new power relations' that were integral to 'the capitalist-liberal state' (Kalyvas 2002: 117) it was still marked by a refusal to interpret 'this materiality of power (and thus of the state) as rooted in the relations of production and social division of labour' (Poulantzas 1978: 67). However, Foucault did eventually start to grapple with some of these questions in his later work, where the focus was on how some technologies of power were selected over others, and then brought together in stable ensembles and strategies of government (ibid.: 151; see also Jessop 2008: Chapter 6). As part of this shift, Foucault also increasingly engaged with the existence of 'a general line of force that traverses the local oppositions and links them together' (Foucault 1990: 94; cf. Jessop 2008: 153).

Nevertheless, Foucault remained profoundly vague about what the general line that traverses the 'micro-diversity of power relations' is actually grounded in and congealed from (Jessop 2008: 140, 148, 152-153). And it is precisely this silence that resurfaces in the inability of Foucauldian ethnographies of state-society relations to sufficiently grasp how a determinate form of state will be constituted in such a way as to structurally constrain the advance of subaltern political projects through its institutional ensemble.

Thus my contention is this: in order to adequately grasp the dialectic of conjunctural opportunities and structural constraints in subalterns' encounters with state power, it will be necessary to fuse our ethnographic attentiveness to the situated and everyday aspects of state-society relations with a historical awareness of the macro-structural dynamics of capitalist development and state formation as 'master change processes' (Tilly 1982: 44). This in turn takes us towards the domain of historical sociology and a concern with how '[the] shaping of action by structure and transforming of structure by action both occur as processes in time' (Abrams 1982: 6).

Towards a Historical Sociology of State-Society Relations in the Study of Subaltern Politics

In this part of the chapter, I move on to address the challenge of constructing a conceptual approach that is capable of grasping how, on the one hand, subaltern politics is always-already imbricated in state-society relations, and how, on the other hand, state-society relations simultaneously enable and constrain subaltern politics. I do so by elaborating the reading of Gramsci that I presented in chapter 1 through a dialectical rethinking of subalternity and hegemony that focuses on the nature of contestation in and through the lattice-work of 'connective tissues' (Gramsci 2001: 102) between subaltern and dominant groups that is mediated by 'the integral state' (Gramsci 1998: 239).

Subalternity, Fields of Force, and Hegemony

If we want to restore a dialectical sensibility to our understanding of subaltern politics, we need to start by rethinking subalternity itself as a determinate positionality within a set of historically constituted relations between social groups that are differentially situated and endowed in terms of 'the extent of their control of social relations and ... the scope of their transformative powers' (Sewell 1992: 20). Subalternity, then, must be related to the moulding, over time, of 'a societal 'field-of-force'' (Thompson 1978: 151) through the contentious unfolding of 'hegemonic processes' (Mallon 1994: 70).[10]

In trying to understand subalternity and hegemony in these terms, it is imperative to recall that Gramsci (1998: 182) thought of the construction of 'the hegemony of a fundamental social group over a series of subordinate groups' as a gradual process. Through such processes, dominant or ascendant social groups develop political projects that enable them to gain the consent of subaltern groups 'to the general direction' (ibid.: 12) that they seek to impose on social life. Subaltern consent, however, can only be gained through 'a continuous process of formation and superseding of 'unstable equilibria ... between the interests of the fundamental group and those of the subordinate groups' (ibid.: 182). Thus, hegemony will bear the imprint of this: as a result of the making of concessions, what emerges from a hegemonic process is necessarily 'an always dynamic or precarious balance ... among contesting forces' (Mallon 1994: 70).

How do we then understand the positionality and agency of subaltern groups within such fields of force?[11] 'Subaltern groups', Gramsci (1998: 182) argued, 'are always subject to the activity of ruling groups, even when they rebel and rise up ...'. What he meant by this is that subaltern agency—ranging from everyday negotiations of the workings of power from above to collective action challenging adverse incorporation into a social formation[12]—will tend to proceed by engaging institutional ensembles, framing claims through discourses, and mobilizing through political forms that are commensurable with and geared towards the reproduction of unequal structures of power. This is in turn a result of the fact that the compromises that have been struck in and through hegemonic processes remain ones 'in which the interests of the dominant social groups prevail' (ibid.: 182): subaltern groups are positioned in relation to socioeconomic relations, political institutions and cultural forms that, despite concessions and compromises, buttress the reproduction of hegemony. Consequently, subaltern resistance is conditioned by and mediated through 'the social condensations of hegemony' (Morton 2007: 92).

Gramsci conceived of the development of oppositional projects from below as a trajectory in which subaltern groups strive to develop political strategies and forms that will better enable them 'to transform their subordinate social positions' (Green 2002: 15). The starting point of this trajectory is always the 'objective formation' of a given subaltern group as the result of the reorganization of a determinate social formation—in other words, capitalist development and state formation as master change processes. From this starting point, Gramsci conceives of the articulation of subaltern politics in terms of attempts to move from an active or passive affiliation to 'dominant political formations' that have been developed 'to secure the assent of the subaltern groups and to maintain control over them' (Gramsci 1998: 52).

Initially, these attempts will take the form of limited claims and demands, but the experience of impasses in the pursuit of these claims may prompt the development of political organizations that press for more comprehensive, autonomous claims—albeit within the parameters of the extant social and political order. Finally, subaltern groups may move towards the development of genuinely counterhegemonic projects that assert their 'integral autonomy' (ibid.: 52) against the dominant social groups and aim for thoroughgoing systemic transformation. Crucially, Gramsci does not posit the unfolding of this trajectory as a teleological necessity. Rather, the tendency towards unification that exists in the collective agency of subaltern groups 'is continually interrupted by the activity of the ruling groups' (ibid.: 55) and therefore cannot be taken for granted. With these foundations in place, the next step is to consider the role of state formation in hegemonic processes and subaltern politics.

Subalterns and State Formation in Hegemonic Processes

The construction of hegemony, in Gramsci's view, is intrinsically linked to state formation and the workings of state power: it is in and through the state that dominant groups ultimately articulate and gain consent for hegemonic projects, which in turn enable them to give form and direction to trajectories of social change (Gramsci 1998: 52).

In opposition to liberal conceptions that compartmentalize the different regions of social formations, Gramsci (1998: 263) argued that 'State = political society + civil society, in other words hegemony protected by the armour of coercion'. Political society is constituted by '[t]he apparatus of state coercive power which "legally" enforces discipline on those groups who do not "consent" either actively or passively' (ibid.: 12)—or, as Peter Thomas (2009: 137) has put it, 'the machinery of government and legal institutions.' Civil society, on the other hand, is the sphere in which 'the spontaneous consent' of subaltern groups is organized and reproduced through 'the ensemble of organisms commonly called "private"' (Gramsci 1998: 12)—such as schools, religious institutions, and trade unions (see Buttigieg 1995). And Gramsci (1998: 239) coined the term 'the integral state' to denote 'the unity of the moments of civil society and political society' (Thomas 2009: 157).

The notion of the 'integral state' is significant for our understanding of the construction of hegemony because it denotes a distinctive feature of modern processes of state formation, namely 'an increasingly more sophisticated internal articulation and condensation of social relations within a given state form' (Thomas 2009: 140). A crucial part of this is the increasing orientation of the state in capitalist modernity towards the construction of relationships between dominant and subaltern groups (see Thomas 2013: 27-28). In contrast to previous ruling groups, dominant groups under capitalism seek 'to construct an organic passage from the other classes into their own' (Gramsci 1998: 260) through a state that operates through institutions, discourses and technologies of rule that achieve the 'capillary and permanent direction of an entire social fabric ...' (Burgio, cited in Thomas 2009: 144; see also Morton 2007: 92-3).

The converse side of the centrality of the integral state to the working out of hegemonic projects from above is of course its centrality as a modality through which oppositional politics is articulated and pursued by subaltern social groups. Two points are vital in this respect: one relates to the contradictions of 'moral regulation' (Corrigan and Sayer 1985) in processes of state formation; the other to how the state as 'a *site* and a *centre* of the exercise of power' (Poulantzas 1978: 148) is constituted in ways that ultimately undergird the reproduction of hegemonic structures of power.

The Contradictions of Moral Regulation: It is precisely because of the construction of organic passages between dominant and subaltern social groups that state formation as a master change process comes to articulate with the 'local rationalities' (Nilsen 2009; Nilsen and Cox 2013) that animate subaltern politics. State formation is a profoundly cultural process, predicated on forms of 'moral regulation' that are geared towards encouraging some ways of organizing social life 'whilst suppressing, marginalizing, eroding, and undermining others' (Corrigan and Sayer 1985: 4). An integral aspect of this regulation is the emphasis put on unification: 'Centrally, state agencies attempt to give unitary and unifying expression to what are in reality multifaceted and differential historical experiences of groups within society, denying their particularity' (ibid: 4).

This is achieved partly through totalizing idioms of loyalty and identity tied to nationalism, and partly through individualizing projects that register people within the state as citizens, taxpayers and so on and so forth. Thus, one can think of the 'organic passage' that dominant social groups seek to build between themselves and subaltern social groups through the integral state as being constructed by projects of moral regulation. In this way, 'subaltern classes are intertwined with processes of state formation' (Morton 2007: 62). Indeed, the emphasis on the unification and erasure of particularity and systematic inequality in processes of modern state formation is precisely the defining feature of civil society as a moment of the integral state (Thomas 2009: 144).

The crucial point, however, is that the moral regulation of the state does not proceed untrammelled and without contestation. There will, unavoidably, be scope for dissonance to arise between the 'unifying representations' that are at the heart of bourgeois state formation and actual lived experiences of 'inequality, domination and subordination' (Corrigan and Sayer 1985: 6). As a result of this dissonance, the 'universalizing vocabularies' of the modern state do not merely serve as pillars of hegemony, but also become 'sites of protracted struggle as to what they mean and for whom' as subaltern groups mobilize to contest their adverse incorporation in a given social formation (ibid.: 7, 6; see also Nugent and Alonso 1994: 211).

In this sense, then, popular struggles 'do not take up a position absolutely external to power: they are always an integral part of the power edifice and make their own mark on the state by reason of its complex articulation with the totality of power mechanisms' (Poulantzas 1978: 151; see also Joseph and Nugent 1994: 20).

The Structuring of the State: The state in its 'integral form' has to be understood not as 'a sovereign instance above civil society' but as 'a network of social relations for the production of consent, for the integration of the subaltern classes into the expansive project of historical development of the leading social group' (Thomas 2009: 143, 343). This is highly significant in terms of understanding the equations of conjunctural opportunities and structural constraints in subaltern engagements with the state. As I argued above, the social relations that undergird hegemony are not shaped by the unilateral exercise of power by dominant social groups, but through a trajectory of contentious negotiations that culminates in a 'compromise equilibrium' in which 'account is taken of the interests and the tendencies of the groups over which hegemony is to be exercised ...' (Gramsci 1998: 161).

Now, given its ontological moorings in these relations, it also follows that the state 'above all is the condensation of a relationship of forces defined precisely by struggle' (Poulantzas 1978: 151). This means that within a given structuration and institutionalization of state power there will always be 'internal limits imposed by the struggles of the dominated' (ibid.: 151). And, crucially, it is these limits that generate conjunctural opportunities for subaltern groups to pursue their political projects via the modalities of state power. Yet, it remains the case that the compromise equilibrium that makes hegemony possible 'cannot touch the essential' (Gramsci 1998: 161). The equilibrium, after all, sustains the hegemonic position of the dominant social group. The consequence of this is the simple but important fact that '[t]he state is an ensemble of power centres that offer unequal chances to different forces within and outside the system to act for different political purposes' (Jessop 2008: 37). Bob Jessop (1990, 2008) has referred to this as the 'strategic selectivity' of the state—a selectivity that is manifest in the greater ease with which dominant social groups are able to use the state in their pursuit of hegemonic projects and, on the other hand, the structural constraints faced by subaltern social movements as they seek to harness the state to oppositional projects.

Thus, when we study the ways in which subaltern groups pursue oppositional projects in relation to the state, the key challenge is to delineate *both* the enablements *and* the constraints that characterize such processes in specific contexts and particular scales. For a historical-sociological approach to the study of subaltern politics, this means that it will be necessary to trace the origins of a particular structuring of a determinate form of state to previous cycles of contestation and struggle between dominant and subaltern groups. And to extend this analysis in a politically relevant direction, it will be necessary to develop grounded understandings of what subaltern groups can achieve by appropriating the institutions, discourses, and technologies of rule of the state, while simultaneously raising questions about how oppositional projects from below can destabilize and rupture the structures of social power from which the state is ultimately congealed.

In the context of contemporary India, the need for such an approach is arguably particularly urgent. On the one hand, recent years have witnessed the deepening of Indian democracy through the emergence of what Ruparelia (2013) calls 'the new rights agenda'—that is, national rights-based legislation to secure civil liberties and socioeconomic entitlements—and an increasing tendency of subaltern politics to be oriented towards socio-legal activism. On the other hand, Indian democracy is at the same time being hollowed out by an elite-led process of neoliberal restructuring that has thrown up new forms of uneven development and has failed to enhance the life chances of India's subaltern populations (see Nilsen and Roy 2015). In this conjuncture, knowing 'what is to be done' will by necessity mean knowing something about what to do in relation to the state.

Notes

1. This should of course not be read as an argument that the colonial state was founded on liberal principles. As Kaviraj (2010b: 60) notes, the colonial state was profoundly authoritarian. The problem, however, in Kaviraj's account is that he overlooks how the modern western state too was only democratized gradually, through popular mobilization that challenged the reactionary alliance of aristocracies with ascendant bourgeoisies that emerged after the revolutionary convulsions of 1848 (Halperin 2004; Silver 2003).
2. Similarly to Kaviraj, Guha arguably operates with a caricatured view of the development of the bourgeois state in the metropolitan context, in which the popular classes are seen as always-already incorporated into its ambit as citizens with democratic rights (see footnote 2 above; see also Chibber 2013).
3. See Nilsen (2011) for an engagement with Fuller and Harris (2001) and Corbridge et al. (2005).
4. See also Gupta (2012: Chapter 3).
5. The literature on governmentality is too vast to summarize here. See Foucault (2007 and 2008) for the original statements of the idea and Rose (1999) and Dean (2009) for instructive discussions.
6. See also Gupta (2012: Chapter 7).
7. A similar argument can be found in the work of Sumi Madhok (2013) who has focused on the Women's Development Programme in Rajasthan, a forerunner to MS. Because of space constraints, I do not engage with her work in this chapter.
8. See e.g. Duschinski (2009) and Baruah (1999) on the use of direct military force in Kashmir and the North-East; Sundar (2006, 2007, 2010) on the use of paramilitary outfits like the Salwa Judum in response to the Maoist insurgency in Bastar; Kumar (2008) on the use of landlord armies against militant Dalits as 'surrogate arms of the state'; and Menon and Nigam (2007) and Pati (2006) on state violence against democratic resistance to displacement.
9. I owe this point to Alpa Shah's comments on Akhil Gupta's book in "Thinking Allowed: Family Funerals; Red Tape", which aired on BBC Radio 4 on December 3, 2012 (http://www.bbc.co.uk/programmes/b01p0hnv). See also Harriss and Jeffery (2013).
10. See Roseberry (1994) for a set of instructive comments on Thompson's concept of field of force.
11. See Green (2011) for a profoundly instructive reading of the richness of Gramsci's notion of the 'subaltern'.
12. See Nilsen (2009) and Nilsen and Cox (2013) for a discussion of the different phases and forms of 'movement processes' from below.

Part II

Popular Struggles in Contemporary India

3

Against the Current, from Below
Resisting Dispossession in the Narmada Valley

"Before our village was submerged, we would eat four *rotis*[1] four times a day; now we eat two *rotis* two times a day": this is how Chetram Narte, a Gond Adivasi peasant, described the impact of the Bargi dam on the livelihoods of the villagers of Piparya on the upper reaches of the Narmada river in eastern Madhya Pradesh.[2] The Bargi dam is one of the more than 3,000 dams making up the Narmada Valley Development Project (NVDP)—a river basin development project that seeks to harness the waters of the Narmada river as it winds its way from the Maikal ranges in Amarkantak in Shahol district of Northern Madhya Pradesh to the Arabian Sea at Bharuch, Gujarat.[3] Prior to the coming of the dam, Chetram and his family used to farm five acres of land. Now, however, they are left to eke out a living from two acres. For many households in the submergence zone, the loss of land to the reservoir of the Bargi dam, which was completed in 1990, has compelled one or several family members to migrate to regional urban centres in western and central India to find work. In these urban centres, people often work on construction sites, although it is not unusual to find oustees from the Bargi reservoir area pulling rickshaws in the nearby city of Jabalpur (field notes February 2003).

Chetram Narte and his fellow villagers are only some of the many Adivasi peasants who have joined the ranks of India's 645 million poor people as a result of being displaced by large dams. Adivasis constitute some eight per cent of India's population, but 40 per cent of the 20 to 30 million people that have been displaced by large dams since independence (Whitehead 2003). The record of the Indian state on resettlement and rehabilitation (R&R) of people who have lost their livelihoods, lifeworlds and habitats to dams and other large-scale development projects is dismal, and this is the main reason why development-induced displacement more often than not entails impoverishment. Despite the extensive powers of expropriation bestowed upon the state, there is as yet no national legal framework that adequately protects the rights of project-affected persons (PAPs) or lays down uniform national guidelines for the conduct of R&R (Parasuraman 1999; Cernea 1999). As a result, most peasant communities who are dispossessed by the construction of large dams 'find themselves faced with the option of starving to death or walking several kilometres to the nearest town, sitting in the marketplace ... offering themselves as waged labour, like goods on sale' (Roy 2002: 103). In these marketplaces, they become part of a 'surplus population' of rural migrants who have been dispossessed either, like them, by land acquisition for development projects and transnational investments, or by the 'piecemeal dispossession of small-scale farmers, unable to survive when exposed to competition from agricultural systems backed by subsidies and preferential tariffs' (Li 2009: 68, 71; see also Walker 2008). In India, this surplus population scrambles for whatever employment may be available within the context of an economy which, despite sporting impressive growth rates of some 9 per cent for several consecutive years, is characterized by jobless growth and a low capacity for labour absorption (Breman 1996, 2010).

The impoverishment of marginal groups such as Adivasi peasants stands in stark contrast to the enrichment of the groups that Bardhan (1998) has labelled as India's 'dominant proprietary classes'—in particular, capitalist farmers—as a result of the construction of large dams. In terms of the impact of dams on irrigation, the India Case Study Report for the World Commission on Dams argues that this has been 'almost entirely distributional'—that is, actual increases in irrigation and agricultural yields have been systematically overestimated and the benefits actually generated have been cornered by powerful groups in the command areas of the dams, all at the expense of the public and the project-affected people (Rangachari, Sengupta, Iyer, Banerji and Singh 2000: 56-57; see also Klingensmith 2007).

The consistent distributional bias of large dams points to how large dams have been instrumental to a process of 'accumulation by dispossession' (Harvey 2003) which has concentrated property rights in water in the hands of an emergent class of capitalist farmers while generating pressures towards the partial proletarianization of subaltern groups. This dynamic is not unique to India's large dams. Rather, it is linked to a fundamental and generic aspect of the 'passive revolution' that has moulded the political economy of capitalism in postcolonial India (Chatterjee 1993; Kaviraj 1997). In this process, state-led development strategies have resulted in the transfer and concentration of productive resources in such a way as to 'enhance the power of those who were the most important holders of property rights—in the first place, the industrial and commercial bourgeoisie and the rich peasantry—and of the bureaucratic office holders whose discretionary powers were increased with the greatly expanded role of the bureaucracy as a whole' (Corbridge and Harriss 2000: 65).

This process, however, has not proceeded without contestation from below. Since the 1970s, a new wave of popular movements has emerged in India to contest the dispossessory and exploitative dynamics of state-led capitalist development (Omvedt 1993; Vanaik 1990). In the Narmada Valley, this has taken the form of a militant anti-dam campaign—the Narmada Bachao Andolan (NBA; Save the Narmada Movement)—that unfolded from the middle of the 1980s until the present. Central to the collective action of the NBA was the attempt to stop the Sardar Sarovar Project (SSP), the kingpin of the NVDP, which is intended to furnish irrigation and electricity for the economically prosperous and politically powerful region of central Gujarat (Nilsen 2010: Chapter 2). The campaign ultimately failed when, in 2000, India's Supreme Court ordered that the project should be completed. However, as one of India's most significant and substantial movements against displacement over the past three decades, the trajectory of the NBA and its strategies of resistance holds important insights, particularly at a time when neoliberal reform in India is producing ever-more aggressive threats to the livelihoods of the country's subaltern groups and popular classes—whether in the form of Special Economic Zones, mining projects, agrarian crisis, or urban restructuring in the country's mega-cities (Banerjee-Guha 2008; Padel and Das 2010; Walker 2008; Banerjee-Guha 2011). In this chapter, I put forward an analysis of the Narmada Bachao Andolan as a 'movement process' (Nilsen 2009), in which activists continually developed multiple forms of materially grounded and locally generated skilled activities around a rationality that opposed the hegemonic projects of dominant social groups. The analysis attempts to unearth and understand the ways in which activists seek to realize the contingent potentiality for expanding the scope and aims of their oppositional projects, and the enablements and constraints they are confronted with in this process (Nilsen 2009).

Discovering the Dam: Militant Particularisms in the Narmada Valley, 1985-87

Maharashtra: The Narmada Dharangrasta Samiti

It is Adivasis, the historian Ramachandra Guha (2007: 3305) has recently argued, who 'have gained least and lost most from six decades of democracy and development in India'. This is certainly true for the communities of Bhil and Bhilala Adivasis[4] that stand to be affected by the SSP across the states of Maharashtra, Madhya Pradesh, and Gujarat. Grinding poverty combines with abysmal literacy rates and grim health indicators in a region characterized by the failure of subsistence agriculture to yield an adequate livelihood. This results in pervasive and large-scale migration to the prosperous agrarian and industrial regions of South and Central Gujarat to find work (Mosse, Gupta and Shah 2005).

The impact of socio-economic marginalization has been compounded by political disenfranchisement. In the Adivasi communities, local state-society relationships are profoundly undemocratic, and characterized by what I have referred to elsewhere as 'everyday tyranny' (Nilsen 2010: Chapter 3). Everyday tyranny essentially revolved around local state officials—police constables and forest rangers—exacting bribes, both in cash and in kind, from Adivasis in order to turn a blind eye to their customary yet formally unlawful use of state-owned forests for cultivation, timber and fuel collection, and other related livelihood activities. Demands for bribes were in turn underpinned by a very real threat of violence: if local police officers discovered a villager walking along the road carrying an axe or a sickle, they would often bring the person to the police outpost where he would be beaten up and then made to pay a bribe in order to avoid criminal charges (interviews and fieldnotes, March 2003). Whatever the resentment that may have simmered beneath the surface, fear of violence and reprisals meant that villagers responded to the exactions of the local representatives of the state with deference and submission, which in turn thwarted any capacity on their part to make rights-based claims of any kind on the state in order to address their poverty and exclusion (Nilsen 2010: Chapter 3). As the emergence of the Narmada Dharangrasta Samiti in the dam-affected communities in Akkalkuwa and Akrani *tehsils* in the district of Nandurbar in Maharashtra illustrates, the building of the first militant particularisms in response to the SSP also entailed challenging everyday tyranny.

Keshuvbhai is one of the most senior activists from the dam-affected Adivasi communities of Maharashtra. This is how he depicted the situation in the villages prior to 1985:

> The villagers had heard that there was a dam coming up in Gujarat and had been told that they would get compensation in the form of land for land. The authorities claimed that their lives would improve. They were told that the Sardar Sarovar would bring great benefits: it would yield massive gains in electricity and irrigation;

> thousands of villages that had been in darkness would be lit, and villages that were without proper water supplies would now have water. They didn't question these claims, nor did they inquire about how the dam would impact their community in particular; they conceived of the government as an ultimate power which was not to be questioned (interview, March 2003).

Their understanding of the government as all-powerful was linked to the workings of everyday tyranny. They were all too familiar with the coercive and extortive ways of the forest rangers and police officers, and the government's survey teams conducted themselves no differently: when a team of surveyors came to a village, the villagers would typically have to provide pots of home-made liquor and give up their chickens for meals. The team would also demand bribes of 40 to 50 rupees from every household (interview, March 2003). The unaccountability of the state officials also extended to the non-disclosure of information; the communities were largely kept in the dark about the extent and the impact of the impending submergence (Parasuraman 1997).

In 1985, Medha Patkar, an action researcher from the Ahmedabad-based NGO Society for Social Knowledge and Action (SETU), arrived in Nandurbar district to survey the dam-affected communities. Her first impression of the Adivasi communities was one of a lack of information and knowledge about the SSP and its impacts: 'the first two days we walked through the Valley, we realized that people didn't even know about the project ... when we moved through the villages, we realized that there was no information' (interview, June 2003). Keshuvbhai recounted the initial encounters with the outsider as being riddled with scepticism, but this gradually changed as Patkar proved her genuine commitment in practice:

> On one particular occasion, a government surveying team had come to Sikka, a nearby village. As usual, they collected fifty rupees from every household, demanded that the villagers cook them a chicken meal, and got very drunk. Medha showed up in Sikka and took photographs of the ill-mannered officials. The officials got scared and ran away. When they learned about this incident, the villagers came to trust Medha and started telling her about the atrocities they suffered at the hands of state officials (interview, March 2003).

The next step in the process revolved around gathering information about the impacts of the SSP and establishing an organizational structure that would make it possible to articulate grievances and demands and mobilize communities around these grievances and demands. Patkar and a team of young collaborators from SETU and the affected villages gathered the necessary information: official project documents were examined and surveys of the dam-affected villages were carried out in order to establish a yardstick by which to gauge official claims about the costs and benefits of the SSP.

Simultaneously, the need for an organizational structure became evident: 'When it was discussed in three- and four-hour meetings in hamlet after hamlet, it was very clear that the issues were multiple and the people must get channels and access to the right places where they could raise these questions and get the answers' (Patkar 1995: 158). A multi-tiered structure emerged, comprising village-level committees with representatives from each hamlet, block-level committees with representatives from each village, *tehsil*-level committees with representatives from the various blocks, and finally a joint committee for both the affected *tehsils*. Internally, this became a vehicle for discussion and decision-making, and externally it became a vehicle for representation vis-à-vis the dam-building authorities and the state government. The local struggle was embedded in a network of urban support groups, and linked its activities to transnational advocacy networks that campaigned on the issue of indigenous people and development-induced displacement (Khagram 2004). In early 1986, the organization was formalized as the Narmada Dharangrasta Samiti (NDS) and posited the right to information as its principal demand (Patkar 1995).

Madhya Pradesh: Khedut Mazdoor Chetna Sangath

Across the Narmada river, in western Madhya Pradesh, the Adivasi communities of Alirajpur had already been mobilized since the early 1980s by the independent trade union Khedut Mazdoor Chetna Sangath (KMCS; Peasants' and Workers' Consciousness Union). The KMCS had led a relatively successful mobilization against the everyday tyranny of the local state, and had instilled in the communities that it mobilized an awareness of basic democratic rights and the skills needed to collectively claim and protect these rights (Nilsen 2010: Chapter 3; Baviskar 1995: Chapter 8).

In Alirajpur as in Nandurbar, the SSP was shrouded in a lack of information. Although some 26 of the 100 villages mobilized by the KMCS stood to be submerged by the reservoir of the dam, researchers who surveyed the area in the early 1980s found that local people knew 'very little' about the dam, and that 'even less of this is clear information from official sources' (Dhamgawar 1997: 93). Vaniya, an activist from the village of Jhandana, explained that even though the villagers had heard of the dam, they assumed that since the river had been flowing since time immemorial, it couldn't be dammed. And anyway, if the government wanted to build the dam, they would have to let them build it—they knew very well that no one can stop the government (interview, March 4, 2003). However, following the advice of the Gujarat-based social action group ARCH Vahini, which worked with dam-affected Adivasi groups in eastern Gujarat, activists from the KMCS began to probe the implications of the SSP in the mid-1980s. In the process, they met and got to know the activists that were mobilizing the affected communities in Maharashtra, and initiated a dialogue on the issues raised by the impending submergence and displacement (interview, Rahul Banerjee, April 2003).

Gradually within the KMCS the mobilization around the demand for information and adequate resettlement and rehabilitation 'really erupted and took on a life of its own', as some activists devoted more time to mobilizing in the submergence zone in Alirajpur (interview, Chittaroopa Palit, May 2003). Although displacement was not a concern for all the communities mobilized by the KMCS, the organization nevertheless viewed the issue as representative of the way in which the state violated the rights of Adivasi communities, and therefore participated actively in the initial efforts to pressure state authorities to supply the dam-affected communities with relevant information about the SSP and its impacts, and to demonstrate that an adequate strategy for resettlement and rehabilitation had been put in place. As one activist of the KMCS put it, there was never really a hard and fast line between mobilizing in relation to the SSP and the work of the KMCS more generally (interview, Kemat, March 2003).

Gujarat: ARCH Vahini

In the dam-affected Adivasi communities in Gujarat, mobilization started in 1980 under the auspices of ARCH Vahini, a social action group funded by Oxfam to engage in health-related activities in the area (Patel 1995, 1997).

Much as in the case of the NDS and the KMCS, the Vahini activists found that the communities had little or no information about the dam and its implications: 'The tribals knew nothing about the project and their imminent displacement' (Patel 1995: 182). Overcoming scepticism towards outsiders, the Vahini activists started to raise the issue of resettlement and rehabilitation and to construct a working alliance with the communities. The first major conflictual encounter with state authorities occurred in 1983, when households in several villages had started to accept the official resettlement and rehabilitation package offered by the Government of Gujarat (GoG). The Vahini activists viewed this packaged as inadequate as it failed to grant compensation to households living on and cultivating "encroached" land. When the GoG reneged on a written promise of rehabilitation, the Vahini decided to act and took the matter to the Gujarat High Court, which in turn upheld the complaint: 'The effect was dramatic. Through their practical experience, the tribals now came to know that the government was not invincible after all, and that the law could be used to their advantage as well' (Patel 1997: 72).

Another decisive breakthrough for the ARCH Vahini in 1983 was the establishment of contact with the World Bank. The activists drew the Bank's attention to how the rights of encroachers and oldest sons and the right to land-for-land compensation went unrecognized by the

GoG, and in response the Bank initiated an inquiry in the SSP resettlement and rehabilitation policy. The issue of encroachers' rights continued to be significant as the three riparian states and the World Bank entered into negotiations over the SSP Loan Agreement in 1984. The Bank demanded the regularization of encroached holdings and recognition of encroachers' rights to land-for-land compensation, and the riparian states finally had to concede to these demands (Patel 1997: 75). However, the GoG failed to follow up on the guidelines for R&R stipulated in the Loan Agreement, and a new round of contention was sparked off with a major protest at the SSP dam site in early 1985 as well as further action in the Gujarat High Court and the Supreme Court. The conflict kept rolling until 1987, when the World Bank implemented yet another inquiry into the SSP. The Bank mission in turn made it clear that the GoG was bound by law to provide land-for-land compensation to each encroacher and the oldest sons of encroachers. For the Vahini activists, this was a decisive victory which facilitated the creation of a satisfactory policy and strategy for resettlement and rehabilitation (Patel 1997: 76-77).

Again, then, we see how a small-scale subversion of the received wisdoms involved in everyday tyranny was decisive in advancing mobilization. For the ARCH Vahini, this initial concession was followed by more significant gains in terms of improving the resettlement and rehabilitation policy of the GoG. This was to have profound consequences for the relationship of the ARCH Vahini to the anti-dam campaign that crystallized a year later.

Mobilization Spreads: The Narmada Ghati Navnirman Samiti

Significantly, the movement process in the Narmada Valley

has also involved the Hindu agriculturalist communities of the Nimad region of western Madhya Pradesh, which in contrast to the Adivasi communities exhibits a social structure with distinct patterns of caste- and class-based stratification, an economy based on cash crop farming, as well as deep involvement in mainstream party politics. The Nimadi scenario also differs in terms of its history of resistance to the SSP as there have been several rounds of mobilization from the late 1960s and early 1970s onwards. The mobilization that took place in the 1970s aimed to limit the height of the dam to avoid submergence in Nimad, and was deeply implicated in party politics at the state level. The embeddedness in local politics—essentially rivalry between the Congress Party and the Janata Party over the control of votes in the area—also led to its foundering. This in turn came to constitute an impediment to new rounds of mobilization (interview, Sitaram Patidar, April 2003).

Nevertheless, by the mid-1980s veteran Gandhian social workers had formed a new organization in Nimad—the Narmada Ghati Navnirman Samiti (NGNS). The initial impact of the NGNS, however, was limited as their activities were restricted to awareness-raising and attempts at negotiation with the government rather than grassroots mobilization (interview, Mahesh Patel, April 2003). This, however, changed in mid-1987 when the activists of the NDS turned their attention towards the dam-affected communities in Nimad. Medha Patkar recounted how she first encountered Nimadi activists who found themselves at a loss as to how to create a mobilizing momentum: 'I went there and talked, and they said, "we are not able to go to the villages and mobilize, so now there is no work going on, but we have formed this committee"' (interview, June 2003).

There was clearly a lack of the kind of infrastructure of contention that had evolved in the Adivasi communities in Maharashtra, and the initial priority thus became the establishment of an organizational structure of mobilized communities (interview, Medha Patkar, June 2003). Indeed, in their narratives of this period of mobilization, village activists would emphasize how the decisive change that occurred was that of the development and extension of the NGNS as a grassroots organization in the wake of the intervention by Patkar and the NDS. Organization-building was accompanied by a gradual change in the perception that contesting state authorities was a losing game: villagers became aware of their entitlements in terms of resettlement and rehabilitation, and they witnessed confrontations where the critical questions of Patkar and her fellow travellers left state officials without answers (interviews, April 2003). As the long-standing village activist Jaganath Patidar put it, people were gradually convinced that mobilization was both necessary and possible (interview, April 2003).

By the mid-1980s, then, militant particularisms in the form of local social action groups that demanded the right to information and the right to resettlement and rehabilitation in the event of displacement had emerged in the dam-affected communities of the three riparian states, and the SSP was being questioned and scrutinized in terms of its social costs and benefits and environmental impacts. To a large extent, and particularly in the Adivasi communities of the three states, this was predicated upon a transformation of 'local rationalities' (Cox 1999; Nilsen 2009)—that is, a transformation in the way in which subaltern groups make sense of and engage with their adverse incorporation into unequal and oppressive relations of power in a given locale.

In challenging the everyday tyranny of the state, the NDS, the KMCS, and the ARCH Vahini reversed a scenario in which Adivasis were treated as subjects rather than citizens by the state. Initially, these communities lacked the practical skills and cognitive resources to challenge this situation. However, through practical involvement in this contentious process, instigated by the catalytic agency of external activists, the skills and resources that were necessary in order to claim information and accountability from responsible authorities across a variety of spatial scales were crafted and honed. In the caste Hindu farming communities of Nimad, the process was somewhat different. Here, activist efforts revolved around rekindling faith in collective resistance for the right to resettlement and rehabilitation, and sustaining mobilization outside the domain of party politics. An emergent infrastructure of contention that traversed spatial scales enabled activists to engage with opponents and adversaries ranging from local government officials and bureaucrats to the World Bank, and brought these authorities within reach of the collective action of these communities. Crucially, strategic dialogues were taking place between the different groups, enabling them to define common situations and name mutual enemies. Albeit uneven and fractured, this dynamic would in turn give rise to the common strategy and common identity that underpinned the Narmada Bachao Andolan as a pan-state anti-dam campaign.

In many ways, this process resonates with recent perspectives on subaltern empowerment in relation to the Indian state. Fuller and Harriss (2001: 2, 25) have argued that rather than being an entity which is alien and irrelevant to the vernacular lifeworlds of subaltern groups, the postcolonial Indian state 'plays an important role in popular consciousness and understanding' and, furthermore, that 'even the poor, low status and weak can sometimes benefit from their adequately competent manipulation of political and administrative systems'. The emergence of militant particularisms in the Narmada Valley of course altered the role that the state played in popular consciousness and understanding by generating among subaltern groups a capacity 'to engage with the state as citizens, or as members of populations with legally defined or politically inspired expectations' (Corbridge, Williams, Srivastava, and Véron 2005: 18). It raises the wider and crucial question of the extent to which subaltern groups in India may be able to pursue their oppositional projects—such as resistance to dispossession by large dams or similar projects—via the institutions, procedures and discourses of the state. Partial answers to this question will emerge as I now turn to a discussion of the pan-state anti-dam campaign, which, like the militant particularisms that preceded it, was predicated on a strategy that sought to hold the state accountable to its democratic commitments to its citizenry.

"No One Will Move; The Dam Will Not Be Built":[5] The Formation and Trajectory of the Anti-Dam Campaign

Towards Dam Opposition: Confrontational Learning and Counter-Expertise

The declaration of total opposition to the SSP on August 18, 1988 constituted the culmination of a protracted engagement with responsible authorities about the impacts of the project, in which the organizations of the dam-affected communities in the Valley demanded the disclosure of information about the extent of submergence and displacement and the status of plans for resettlement and rehabilitation of the dam-affected communities. This occurred in a context of increasing urgency, as the Ministry of Environment and Forests (MoEF) had given conditional clearance for the construction of the SSP to proceed in June 1987.

In November 1987, the NDS and the NGNS submitted a joint memorandum to the Narmada Control Authority (NCA),[6] putting forward a list of demands concerning rehabilitation and information; it warned that unless answers were forthcoming before December 15, a large-scale movement would be inaugurated to put pressure on the NCA (Dwivedi 1997: 10). Spurred on by the reticence of the responsible authorities, a public rally attended by 4,000 dam-affected people was staged in the SSP project-colony in Kevadia, Gujarat to raise issues of displacement and resettlement in January 1988. However, once again the demands for information and dialogue that emanated from the rally were stonewalled: the activists were still denied access to information about these issues. By May 1988, there was a widespread impression among activists that the SSP had not been through a satisfactory project proposal, and the organizations involved called another meeting to discuss these issues among themselves and with representatives of the NCA, the riparian state governments, and central authorities. Medha Patkar (1995: 162) sums up the result of the event: 'After that meeting, we signed a common letter saying that we were giving the government two months' time, and if they did not answer all the questions in two months, we would oppose the project'. Once again, however, the state governments and bureaucratic agencies responded with silence, and this produced the promised result: 'We will stop Sardar Sarovar! We will die, but will not move out; we will not leave the Narmada Valley' (NBA 1988: 196).

Arguably, the move towards dam opposition is exemplary of how social movement politics are radicalized through conflictual encounters with opponents (Barker and Cox 2002). For the organizations of the dam-affected communities, their confrontations with state authorities came to constitute a body of experience which gave rise to a particular understanding of the conflict in which they were immersed and their opponent in the conflict. This in turn led to new answers being given to the fundamental question that activists continually ask themselves: what is to be done?

Indeed, when I asked village activists about how they arrived at the decision to move from claims for adequate information and resettlement to opposing the dam *tout court* they would typically reply that "the government couldn't answer our questions, so we became convinced that they could not resettle us" (interviews and field notes, March/April 2003). What occurred in this process of confrontational learning was partly a shedding of illusions and partly a confirmation of suspicions about the character of state and project authorities and their capacity and willingness to conduct proper R&R. Furthermore, the nature of the process also provided a justification for the radicalization that took place. Recounting the events of 1988, the NBA's official declaration of opposition to the SSP emphasizes how the organizations of the affected groups had set out on a rightful quest for dialogue with the state governments, but encountered reticence and unconvincing responses:

> All have expected that government would implement in an integrated manner the common resettlement policy for all three states, with necessary government machinery and land and other resources with the co-operation of

> the oustees ... The discussion once again made it clear that the state governments have no policy or resources for the oustees (NBA 1988: 194).

The underlying argument is clear: rightful claims were pursued through established channels but yielded nothing other than the knowledge that this pursuit was a dead end; in light of this, activists had no choice but to opt for more radical stances and strategies.

Closely related to this dynamic of confrontational learning was an important process of knowledge production. In a context where state authorities refused to divulge information, activists themselves had to gather and process information about the SSP in terms of its social costs and benefits, its environmental impacts, and plans for resettlement and rehabilitation. This process revolved partly around the examination of official documents pertaining to the project, partly around the surveying of dam-affected communities, and partly around the incorporation of critical appraisals of the project generated by actors external to the movement (Dwivedi 2006). The examination of official documents led to the identification of serious shortcomings and errors in the planning and appraisal of the SSP, and the surveying of dam-affected communities provided the basis for questioning and challenging the responsible authorities and their claims about the project. The outcome was a body of knowledge that can usefully be referred to as counter-expertise (Skirbekk 1984).

According to NBA activist Shripad Dharmidhikary, this counter-expertise added momentum and weight to the conclusions drawn from interactions with state governments and the dam bureaucracy: 'more and more facts came to light, and the enormity of the environmental impacts became clear, as well as our realization that the very rationale of the project—the project benefits—were highly doubtful. All this led us to challenge the project itself' (cited in Fisher 1995: 23). I shall review the various facets of the NBA's counter-expertise as presented in one of the most comprehensive statements of its politics, *Towards Just and Sustainable Development* (NBA 1992).

The first point of criticism concerns the design and planning of the project as such. It is claimed that this was carried out without adhering to official rules regarding impact assessments, and without the level of transparency that ensures a participatory planning process (pp. 5-6). This, it is argued, is expressive of the democratic deficit which dogs the Indian polity and which violates the '[r]ight to know and right to participate meaningfully' (p. 6). Next the claimed benefits of the project—irrigation, electricity, and the provision of drinking water—are carefully reviewed, and it is argued that official claims about benefits are systematically overestimated, and, furthermore, that the benefits that are actually generated are systematically arrogated to dominant groups in Southern and Central Gujarat. The SSP, the argument goes, is justified on the basis of a 'mirage of benefits' (p. 5). The document then proceeds to demonstrate how, conversely, the scale of displacement is grossly underestimated (p. 16). This is related to the fact that a number of dam-affected groups are left out of the official definition and estimation of 'project-affected people'. This criticism is simultaneously quantitative—it pinpoints inaccuracies flowing from inadequate appraisal—and qualitative—it challenges the boundaries of the administrative categories of the state.

The next point to be addressed is the prospects for resettlement and rehabilitation, which are claimed to be nothing short of dismal as 'no comprehensive plan with the details of required land, infrastructure, time frame, allocations and the required political will is in the sight' (p. 17). The 'impossibility of resettlement' is designated as an explicit breach of constitutional rights which raises the broader issue of whether it is possible to justify the erasure of habitation, livelihood and lifeworld. The document then moves on to criticize the financial workings of the project (p. 21). Evidence is presented that shows that the SSP fails to meet the official cost-benefit ratio that has been stipulated for dam projects, and it is argued that the project will inevitably lead to a financial crunch as it must be underwritten by lending. This scenario is posited as an immoral 'daylight robbery' of public resources—the funds are funnelled to a project with an extreme social bias—in a context of severe fiscal problems (India faced a severe balance of payments crisis in the early 1990s). Finally, the document raises the environmental impacts of the project (p. 23) by highlighting how the SSP was given environmental clearance in spite of the fact that an environmental impact assessment had not been carried out.

In the NBA's anti-dam campaign, this body of counter-expertise has functioned as a discourse of resistance which challenges the attempts of dominant groups to legitimate their hegemonic projects 'as being the motor force of a universal expansion, of a development of all the "national" energies' (Gramsci 1998: 182).

Firstly, at the level of the specific campaign against the SSP, the rationale of the project is challenged on its own terms by the presentation of scientific knowledge that stands in contradiction to the official claims about the costs and benefits of the project. Beyond the 'factual' critique, in turn, there is a normative critique that shows how negligent and opaque planning procedures and the social bias in the distribution of costs and benefits violates the officially sanctioned rights and entitlements of the dam-affected communities. Secondly, this critique strikes at the very heart of the strategy through which ideological legitimacy has been sought for development planning in India, namely positing planning as an essentially apolitical 'technical evaluation of alternative policies and the determination of choices on scientific grounds' (Chatterjee 1993: 201) for the good of the nation at large. Pointing out the shortcomings and flaws of the expert knowledge that provides the rationale of a development project such as the SSP and justifying this with reference to scientific standards amounts to a destabilization of the status of expert knowledge in terms of its quality. Pointing out the systematically skewed distribution of the costs and benefits of the project exacerbates this destabilization by calling into question the claimed objectivity of development planning and the extent to which it is dedicated to a generic 'greater common good'. The net effect is to reveal how planning has served as 'a modality of power outside the immediate political process itself' (ibid: 202).

As a discourse of resistance, counter-expertise also has an internal function in relation to the dynamics of the movement process itself. The building of a campaign revolves around bringing together a range of militant particularisms around a generic challenge to a common problem. This is done at two levels in the NBA's counter-expertise. Firstly, the critique is formulated at a pan-state level, drawing together the situations and experiences of dam-affected communities in Gujarat, Madhya Pradesh, and Maharashtra, and abstracting a generic situation and a generic challenge from those specific contexts: 'The oustees in Madhya Pradesh and Maharashtra are well-organized and are *challenging their displacement itself ... They have termed the impending displacement as unjust, unjustifiable* and have questioned the very Public Purpose for which they are being forced out of the valley' (NBA 1992: 19).

Secondly, the critique consistently extends beyond itself and links the various problematic aspects of the SSP to wider issues. This is evident in the argument that the socially and environmentally harmful impacts of the SSP are typical of 'all the mega projects' (ibid: 19), that opaque planning is 'but a reflection of the political culture' (ibid: 6) in India, that the social bias of the allocation of costs and benefits is expressive of 'the basic resource matrix of our country' (ibid: 19), and that the financial ramifications of the SSP are morally unacceptable at a time when 'the nation is passing through severe financial crisis' (ibid: 23). In both respects, the NBA's discourse of resistance moves well beyond a 'not-in-my-backyard' stance, and in doing so it pushes towards the joining together of militant particularisms in a campaign that connects subaltern communities in a generalized challenge to the situation they confront. However, this process was also characterized by fractures and fissures between different rationalities among the social actions groups in the three states.

Divergences in the Making of the Anti-Dam Campaign

The ARCH Vahini was not to follow on the path towards total opposition to the SSP. This divergence, in turn, has to be understood in relation to the trajectory of the Vahini's struggle for resettlement and rehabilitation in the dam-affected communities of Gujarat in 1987-88. The decisive moment in this process was the announcement made in December 1987 by the Government of Gujarat that it would implement a policy that recognized the rights of encroachers to R&R. This generated a scenario of highly differentiated circumstances.

The new Gujarat resettlement and rehabilitation policy appeared to provide the opportunities for which groups like ARCH-Vahini had lobbied, though it represented a significant step forward only for those project-affected people willing to resettle in the state of Gujarat. Unfortunately, the Gujarat policy was not matched by similar policies in Madhya Pradesh and Maharashtra, where the Narmada Ghati Nav Nirman Samiti and the Narmada Dharangrast Samiti, respectively, had their constituencies (Fisher 1995: 23). Since then, the ARCH Vahini has concentrated its activities on monitoring the resettlement and rehabilitation of displaced communities in Gujarat.

This divergence testifies to how the immediate parameters set by differing local exigencies impact on the processes of translation between, and abstraction from, militant particularist struggles, and on the ability to construct a generic challenge to a generic problem. This is not a smooth-running process of unification, but rather a complex process of negotiation of specific exigencies and the way in which these exigencies influence activist preferences and choices.

For some activists, the question "what is to be done" is answered with reference to the possibility of gaining tangible concessions on specific issues in the here and now. This is reflected in how a leading activist of the ARCH Vahini, Anil Patel, highlights the gains made by his organization in Gujarat and argues that the social action groups in Maharashtra and Madhya Pradesh 'stopped looking for ... ways to achieve similar policies in their states and started raising doubts about the policy of Gujarat ...' (Patel 1995: 190). He also argues that this shift reflected the criticism of the GoG's policies by urban intellectuals and Western NGOs. Furthermore, he claims that the declaration of opposition to the SSP was 'as sudden as it was total' (ibid: 190). For others, opting for such concessions entails 'winning ha'pennies and losing pounds' and is thus ruled out in favour of a redefinition of the stakes involved in a conflict. Thus Medha Patkar emphasizes how she and others, came to a different conclusion about the significance of the GoG's policy on resettlement and rehabilitation: 'We felt that the few resolutions by one government did not mean much since the issues were much broader. For instance, even on rehabilitation, the issues of all three states should be looked at together' (ibid: 162). Divergences, then, are an integral aspect of the work of going beyond the local and specific, and towards more generic forms of social movement practice.

The anti-dam campaign, however, was an incontrovertible fact. Between 1988 and 1990 the NBA focused on lobbying relevant state authorities. In 1990, with support both at the wider national level, and from an emergent transnational advocacy network, the Andolan altered its strategy to demand that the Government of India (GoI) should order an extensive review of the SSP, assessing its technical feasibility, cost-benefit equations, and its social and environmental impacts; and that during the course of the review, construction on the dam should be halted. This demand was accompanied by the adoption of various forms of non-violent direct action strategies (Nilsen 2010: Chapter 6). In the following section, I present a detailed analysis of the trajectory of this strategy from 1990 to 2000.[7]

The Trajectory of the Anti-Dam Campaign from 1990 to 2000

In March 1990 the NBA organized a roadblock of the Bombay-Agra highway in Madhya Pradesh. Some 10,000 activists blocked traffic for 28 hours, demanding that Sunderlal Patwa's BJP state government implement a review. The Patwa government heeded the activists' demands and declared that not only would it push ahead with review at state level, it would also put forward the demand to the central government. Later the same month a *dharna*—a sit-in demonstration—was organized in Bombay to put similar pressure on Sharad Pawar's Congress government of Maharashtra. In both cases promises were elicited to the effect that a review would be implemented, and that no submergence would take place until land had been identified for resettlement and rehabilitation. However, these promises failed to yield practical results (Jayal 2000).

The demand for review then entered its second phase as frustrated activists upped the ante and shifted their focus to Delhi and V.P. Singh's Janata Dal central government. This was significant, as this was a government 'elected on a mandate of change and with social movement backing' (Omvedt 1993: 274). Indeed, during the campaign for the general election in 1989, Singh had been sympathetic to the cause of the NBA (Jayal 2000). From May 14–18, a sit-in demonstration was staged outside Singh's residence in Delhi. After four days, the activists were invited into the PM's residence to make their case. Singh then agreed to initiate a review of the SSP (Khagram 2004). However, this potential breakthrough was quickly stymied as the Chief Minister of Gujarat, Chimanbhai Patel—political spearhead of the Patidar agro industrialists of South and

Central Gujarat, a staunch supporter of the SSP, and at this point in time a Janata Dal member—intervened with massive counter-rallies, funded by the Gujarat Chamber of Commerce and Industry, demanding a speedy completion of the project. This apparent display of popular support for the SSP and its potential ramifications in terms of the fortunes of electoral politics rattled Singh, who quickly reneged on the promises of review (Khagram 2004).

As Baviskar (1995: 207) has pointed out, the NBA now found itself involved in 'a race against time' as the construction of the SSP was proceeding without impediments. This was the context for one of the NBA's most spectacular and dramatic protest actions: the *Jan Vikas Sangharsh Yatra* (March of Struggle for People's Development). On December 25, 1990, some 6,000 men and women from the dam-affected communities set out from Rajghat, just outside the town of Badwani in Madhya Pradesh, towards the dam site 'to physically stop the work on the dam, by offering peaceful *satyagraha* at the dam site and thereby pressure the government to comprehensively review the SSP' (NBA newsletter 1991, cited in Dwivedi 1997: 14). The march was stopped after six days, at the town of Ferkuwa, on the border between Madhya Pradesh and Gujarat. This became the site for a crucial standoff between the NBA and state authorities. Six activists went on hunger strike as there had been no response to the demand for review. The strike lasted for 21 days, with activists calling off the hunger strike and withdrawing from Ferkuwa on January 28th. The central government announced that it would set up an all-India review panel for the Narmada dams, and the World Bank assured activists that it would implement an independent review. However, as the minority government of Chandra

Shekhar at the centre was dependent on support from Chimanbhai Patel in Gujarat, nothing substantial came of the promise of a review panel in the immediate aftermath of the march (Jayal 2000).

The demand for review by state and central governments lay dormant from early 1992 to the middle of 1993, as activist energies were focused on mobilization in the villages and interaction with the World Bank review team that arrived in the Valley in 1992. The third phase of the demand for review was instigated in 1993, in the wake of the withdrawal of World Bank funding for the SSP. As a leading NBA activist put it, 'a new phase' had begun, 'with the NBA now face to face with the Indian state' (Palit 2003: 88).

When the demand for review was resuscitated, state and central governments again failed to respond. As a reaction, activists of the Andolan launched an indefinite fast in Bombay on June 3, lasting for three weeks until the government announced that it would initiate a review of the SSP. There was, however, no tangible follow-up of this announcement and the NBA posed the ultimatum of *Jal Samparan*: if a review of the SSP was not declared by August 6th a group of activists would drown themselves in the Narmada (Sangvai 2000). Pressures mounted on the central government as the deadline drew near, and on 5 August a statement was issued to the effect that a Five Member Group (FMG) would carry out a review of the project. The Andolan's *Jal Samparan* was called off (Jayal 2000; Khagram 2004).

However, the FMG had its wings clipped before it could fly. As much as the group went ahead with its work, the GoG and the dam-building authorities boycotted the work completely. When the FMG's report was finally made public in December 1994 it lent support to the NBA's criticism of the project, but this was largely without consequences even though there was significant fragmentation at the top: in Gujarat, Chimanbhai Patel had died and, in Madhya Pradesh, the Congress and Digvijay Singh, brandishing a pro-civil society agenda, had won the state elections (Nilsen 2010: 135-142).

The fourth and final phase of the struggle for a review of the SSP started in May 1994, when the Andolan brought a case of public interest litigation before the Supreme Court, claiming that the SSP would result in a violation of people's basic right to life and livelihood and should therefore be stopped (Khagram 2004: 134). In May 1995 the Supreme Court imposed a stay on the dam while it examined the evidence that had been presented (Khagram 2004; Jayal 2000). Several rounds of hearings were held throughout 1995 and 1996, and in February 1997 an indefinite stay was imposed on the construction of the SSP. The Supreme Court's intervention did not go unnoticed among the supporters of the SSP in the legislature: senior Members of Parliament expressing their dismay over the court's alleged meddling in inter-state affairs when, in the hearings of March 1997, the Supreme Court refused to lift the stay first imposed in 1995. The Supreme Court, however, did not budge (Jayal 2000). Nevertheless, the Andolan's turn to the Supreme Court did not fare well in the end. On October 18, 2000, the Supreme Court announced a two to one majority judgement which ruled that the construction of the SSP 'will continue as per the Tribunal' and that '[e]very endeavour shall be made to see that the project is completed as expeditiously as possible' (cited in NBA 2000a: 7, 9). The verdict brought a definite end to the campaign to stop the SSP.

The rationale for demanding that the GoI should implement a full review of the SSP seems to have been firmly rooted in the substantial body of counter-expertise that had emerged since the late 1980s. Citing obvious discrepancies between official norms and regulations and the actual realities of the project in terms of economic costs and the impact of submergence and displacement, Medha Patkar (1995: 170) argues that 'in the context of this overall reality' the best thing to do was 'to challenge the government ... through a democratic process'. A closer consideration of this strategy reveals a lot about the rationality around which the Andolan's anti-dam campaign was constructed.

The demand for a review of the SSP constitutes what Dwivedi (1997: 28) has called 'jury politics'. Jury politics basically revolve around the presentation of a body of evidence about an object of contestation—in this case, a large dam—to a committee of experts and specialists that assess this evidence and then in turn function as a jury in that, based on the assessment of the evidence, they pass judgement on the claims that have been made about the object of contestation. As a strategy it is predicated upon a perception of the state as actually being able to function as jury—that is, as being able to assess and evaluate a body of evidence for or against a given claim in an unbiased way and to pass judgement on the merits of this claim solely on the basis of that evidence.

In explaining the motivation for adopting the demand for review as a key strategy, Medha Patkar refers to the belief that:

> ... when people raised focused issues and declared their commitment, a representative democratic government ... would really respond across the table, possibly via

> neutral moderators as we were proposing or any other mutually agreed-upon process. That is why in March 1990 we had decided not to go on saying, "No dam, no dam" but to propose a definite review process as a way out (1995: 170).

Much the same can be said about the turn to the Supreme Court. The submission of a public interest litigation was in part influenced by a perception of the Supreme Court as an institution that often backed the claims of social movements and other actors engaged in judicial activism (Jayal 2000; Palit 2003). In many ways, this represents a continuation of the rationality that animated the resistance of the militant particularisms from which the movement process in the Narmada Valley originated. As we saw, these were very much predicated upon using the democratic edifice of the Indian state to claim access to livelihoods, information, and resettlement and rehabilitation as a matter of right. What activists did in the anti-dam campaign was to appropriate sets of norms and principles regarding displacement and resettlement, environmental protection, and, ultimately, the basic democratic rights of Indian citizens. They then sought to hold the Indian government accountable to these norms and principles via the institutional mechanisms provided by the postcolonial state.

According to Khagram (2004: 3), anti-dam campaigns are likely to be 'much more effective in democratic institutional contexts' as these 'offer greater opportunities to organize and gain access to decision-making processes'. Yet the trajectory of the Andolan's demand for review—a trajectory Khagram engages with at length[8]—suggests otherwise. I am not arguing that the state operated as a closely sutured behemoth throughout the decade from 1990 to 2000. Indeed, it is quite possible to tease out cracks and fissures in the state-system in the process, for example in the apparent willingness of several Chief Ministers and one Prime Minister to implement reviews. However, the significant dynamic is that of the closing of the ranks that occurred at every juncture when the push—of the dominant proprietary classes and their political representatives—came to shove. The access of activists to decision-making processes was effectively abrogated.

A similar pattern can of course be found in the NBA's engagement with the Supreme Court. Activists were prompted onto the judicial path by the Supreme Court's track record on public interest litigation, and as we saw the Supreme Court refused to lift the stay on the dam in the face of parliamentary discontent. However, all this was effectively brushed aside with the verdict of October 2000. Indeed, this verdict not only states that the SSP should be completed as quickly as possible, it also made it very clear that the Supreme Court was not to serve as an arena for contesting state development strategies: 'It is for the government to decide how to do its job ... It is now well established that the courts, in the exercise of their jurisdiction, will not transgress into the field of policy decision' (cited in NBA 2000a: 3-4). Once again, the ranks of the state-system were closed at a crucial juncture, and the closure favoured the interests of India's dominant proprietary classes.

This warrants some reflection on a question I broached in my discussion of the initial militant particularisms of the dam-affected communities discussed above. I noted that prior to mobilization around the issue of the SSP and the right to information and R&R, the KMCS had conducted a successful struggle against the everyday tyranny of local state officials in Alirajpur. As I have argued at length elsewhere, this struggle was fundamentally predicated on appropriating the 'universalizing vocabularies' (Corrigan and Sayer 1985: 7) of the state—vocabularies of democracy, citizenship, rights and entitlements, and development—and criticizing the radical disjuncture between these vocabularies and the actual practice of the local state (Nilsen 2010: Chapter 3, 2011). This of course demonstrates that there is some potential for empowerment in what Philip Abrams (1988: 82) called the 'state-idea'—the representation of the state as a coherent body politic external to society, which arbitrates in a neutral and unbiased manner in conflicts between equals. This rationality of appropriating the democratic edifice of the Indian state and using it as a basis for criticizing the state's actual conduct carried over into the demands for information and R&R that were articulated between 1985 and 1987, and then to the far more radical anti-dam campaign, which crystallized in the late 1980s. Why did the strategy register less success in this latter case?

The explanation for these divergent outcomes is, I think, quite straightforward. A challenge to the misconduct of local state officials, such as that levelled by the KMCS in its initial years of operation, was something that the higher echelons of the state-system could concede without undermining its own authority and without going against the interests of extra-local proprietary elites. The NBA's campaign against dam-building, however, was first of all directly pitted against the vested interests of the politically powerful proprietary elites of South and Central Gujarat and, secondly, embedded in a generic opposition to dam-building as a development strategy, as well as a critique of the wider model of development of which this strategy was a part. In short, the campaign against the SSP struck against the heart of the dynamic of resource transfer which has characterized India's passive revolution and the role of the state as an integral modality in this process; in so doing the campaign defied 'the permanence of existing structures and relations' (Kamat 2002: 158). In articulating such a demand, the NBA arguably encountered the limits of what subaltern social movements can achieve via the institutions, practices and discourses of the state; I return to discussing the strategic ramifications of this in my concluding remarks.

"We Want Development, Not Destruction":[9] Constructing a Social Movement Project for Alternative Development

Challenging the Postcolonial Development Project

It has been fashionable among critics from poststructuralist and postcolonial quarters to posit India's new social movements as the authors and actors of a political project that simultaneously represents and points towards 'an authentic site of autonomous insurrection beyond development' (Moore 2000: 171). They are, in Escobar's (1995) notorious formulation, engaged in the crafting of 'alternatives to development'. However, as I show in this section, the discourses of resistance that have been articulated in the Narmada Valley suggests that these claims are fundamentally out of sync with realities on the ground.

In conjunction with the monsoon satyagraha[10] of 2000, the NBA staged a celebration of India's Independence Day on August 15. In the Adivasi village of Nimgavhan (Maharashtra), Independence Day began with a flag-hoisting ceremony: Siddharaj Dhadda, a veteran Gandhian and a respected freedom fighter, hoisted both the Indian flag and the NBA's banner alongside each other. Following the hoisting of the flags, a confrontational event erupted. Two teachers were present at the ceremony. These teachers were employed at local state-run schools, but the reality was that their teaching was as absent as the schools they were supposed to be running. Agitated villagers and activists who argued that their vocation amounted to little more than picking up their pay cheques confronted the teachers with strongly worded grievances, while the teachers cringed and tried to defend themselves by arguing that the hills in the area were too steep to climb and that the Adivasi children showed no interest in learning English. This dismal state of affairs was then thrown into sharp relief with the following point on the programme: the congratulation of young Adivasis who had fared well in official schools after first having completed basic schooling in the Andolan's *Jeevan Shalas*—literally 'schools for life' built and run by the Andolan with a curriculum adapted to Adivasi realities.

Following this, the celebrations continued in the nearby village of Domkhedi with the inauguration of a micro-hydel project. A check-dam had been constructed on a small stream adjacent to Domkhedi, which, when combined with a pedal-powered generator, provided electricity to the village for the first time ever. Whereas the SSP threatened to displace the villagers from their lands and produce costly electricity that would only be available to affluent and predominantly urban consumers, here was a dam project controlled and executed at village level that actually had the potential of delivering a tangible improvement in people's lives. A subsequent NBA press release stated: 'Independence Day is so often a celebration of a country's victory over oppression, but in Nimgavhan, it had an additional meaning of the people's continued resistance against the injustice and exploitation within a nation' (NBA 2000b).

Through the celebration of Independence Day, the NBA conveyed a narrative about its political project in which the spirits of the past were conjured up and their names borrowed in an effort to create something that had never yet existed (see Marx 1984: 10). The freedom struggle and the attainment of independence were acknowledged as fundamental events and achievements—the presence of freedom fighters, the unfolding and hoisting of the Indian flag, indeed, the very celebration of Independence Day itself testified to this. However, at the same time it was a narrative of a national project profoundly out of kilter. The 'tryst with destiny', in this narrative, had gone awry; the promises of freedom and development have been hijacked by elite interests and thus betrayed, leaving large sections of the population by the wayside as outcasts. This betrayal was efficiently illustrated by the contrasts evoked in the celebrations: the putrid condition of state schooling versus the vivacity of the *Jeevan Shalas*; the destruction wrought by the SSP versus the benefits brought to local communities by the micro-hydel project. Simultaneously, the focus on the NBA's constructive activities was expressive of a political project of alternative development that resonated far beyond the Narmada Valley. The movement thus projected itself as an agent on a mission to reclaim and reinvent the ideals of freedom and development.

Now, I do not, of course, labour under the misconception that a closely orchestrated protest event and a carefully worded official statement convey a discourse of resistance that reflects a uniform 'collective consciousness' stretching out into every nook and cranny of the Andolan. However, it nonetheless testifies to the fact that the challenge to the totality constituted by India's postcolonial development project is not articulated from 'an originary space of authentic insurgency and insurrectionary otherness' (Moore 2003: 352). Rather, the discourse of resistance has an essentially immanent character: it articulates a critique of India's postcolonial development project by appropriating and inverting the idioms through which legitimacy has been sought for this project. Thus, whereas the discourse of resistance expressed through this insurgent celebration of India's independence day formulates a radical and fundamental critique of the dominant direction and meaning of development in postcolonial India, there is little to suggest a rejection of development as such.

Limits and Challenges: 'Oppositional Populism' and Questions of Grounding

The Andolan's discourse of resistance can aptly be situated within the imaginary that Gupta (1998: 16) refers to as 'oppositional populism'—that is, a 'disputed and contentious redeployment' of 'the rhetoric of development' in popular critiques of state-led development that is fundamentally predicated upon a dichotomic structure that counterpoises a monolithic 'people' to a monolithic 'elite'. The Andolan's discourse of resistance is structured precisely in this way: the actors who will take the social movement project forward are designated as 'the people'—undifferentiated by class, gender, caste, ethnicity or other structures of stratification and differentiation: 'the larger issues of the alternate model of development become concretized, relevant within the lives of the people and raised by and through the people' (NBA 1992: 29). Conversely, the prevailing direction of development is criticized for only having served the interests of India's elites and for being sustainable only 'on the basis of the partnership between the powerholders in this land and their multinational moneylenders and other allies' (ibid: 2-3).

However, this oppositional populism is also problematic in certain respects. This is because the conception of a homogeneous 'people' that carries forth a project of alternative development against 'the elite' does not match the Andolan's social base, in that there are long-standing conflictual relations between Adivasi communities and caste Hindu communities, and in that the Nimadi farming communities are criss-crossed by class and caste divisions.

In Nimad, the landowning castes—predominantly Patidars by caste—have been at the frontline of the anti-dam campaign. Their representation of the fault lines of the conflict tends to be one that pits socially harmonious rural communities of the Narmada Valley against the powerful coalition of urban industrialists, politicians and transnational capital. Whereas some representatives of the landowning castes would admit that a 'feudal mentality' was still prevalent among sections of the powerful groups in the villages, they would still insist that relationships between castes had become far more egalitarian than had been the case in previous times (interviews and field notes, April-May 2003; see Nilsen 2010: Chapter 7).

At the opposite end of the caste-class spectrum, a different view was offered: landless labourers, most of whom are Dalits, reported that practices of untouchability still existed in the villages, and that their wages were far below the minimum level stipulated by the state. This was in turn paralleled by their marginal participation in the mobilization process. For them, participating in the movement meant going to rallies and demonstrations. However, they had not been a part of decision-making processes or been consulted about the Andolan's strategies. Whenever there was a mass action where their participation was required, an announcement would be made from the temple, and work would be stopped for the day. They had never interacted directly with the NBA leadership; only local activists would sometimes come to their houses. They all categorically rejected the claim that relationships between the caste groups had improved in the wake of mobilization (field notes, April 2003).

Now, the obfuscation of conflictual difference in the Andolan's mass base does of course make good sense in terms of the strategic concerns of the anti-dam campaign. Working against all odds in the first place, it was a crucial and necessary achievement to bring together diverse communities between and within which there were multiple opposing interests and abundant potential for conflict: inter- and intra-group divisions were sidelined in the struggle against a common threat. Still, the uneasy question of Nimad's socioeconomic structure does not simply go away. The conflictual differences that criss-cross these communities might resurface as constraints upon the development of a movement project in which social justice is a central ambition. This is so in that claims for social justice cannot simply be directed outward; they are equally valid vis-à-vis relations and practices of caste and class internal to and between the communities united in their opposition to an external enemy.

Making social justice an actuality through 'the transformation of productive inequalities' and 'the dismantling of disenfranchising social hierarchies' (Moore 2003: 203) in turn clearly runs counter to the vested interests of dominant groups in these communities. This can be considered as the point at which the limits of the 'oppositional populism' that characterizes the Andolan's movement project for alternative development emerge. To act on this—to raise internal critiques and further the capacity of subaltern groups within the community to mobilize autonomously around such issues—is uncomfortable in the sense that it is likely to destabilize and disintegrate extant movement formations. Not to act on it, though, constitutes a lapse into a romanticized conception of 'the local' and 'the community' which effectively silences the plight of those most exploited and oppressed. Such a lapse would constitute an abdication of the ambition of social justice.

A social movement project revolves not only around the articulation of a challenge to the social totality; it also revolves around the building of a capacity for hegemony—i.e. an ability to lead the skilled activity of different social groups in a challenge to the hegemonic projects of dominant social groups. A capacity for hegemony is in turn predicated upon the extent to which a social movement project has achieved a solid grounding in the communities that it claims to represent.

The NBA has been at the forefront of attempts to unite social movements across India around a politics of alternative development. According to Medha Patkar, activists felt the need to establish such an alliance in order to provide local movements with a support network that could provide help when, for example, these movements came under threat from state repression (interview, June 2003). However, the construction of alliances quickly became a more encompassing project aimed at evolving institutions that could articulate a political agenda that went beyond specific struggles and into which specific struggles would in turn be integrated. It is from this process that the National Alliance of People's Movements (NAPM) emerged. Its origins can be traced back to the early 1990s and a context characterized by the onset of neoliberal restructuring and the rise of Hindu communalism in India; it formally came into being in 1996, in the aftermath of an activist tour of fourteen states in India. With more than 100 organizations as official members, the NAPM is today deeply involved in the mounting struggles against land acquisition and dispossession as a result of Special Economic Zones and mining projects.

However, the crucial question is the extent to which an alliance such as the NAPM and its politics of alternative development is actually embedded in the local communities it claims to represent. What struck me during my fieldwork was that the movement alliances that had been formed seemed to be remote from the lived experiences of village activists. When I asked activists in the Adivasi villages whether they were familiar with the NAPM, they would typically answer that they did not participate much in those activities; some even claimed that they had not heard of these organizations (interviews and field notes, March and April 2003). Thus, while the formation of an alliance such as the NAPM represents a crucial achievement in terms of moving towards the articulation of a challenge to India's postcolonial development project, this alliance and the challenge it poses do not seem to be experienced as immediately significant by those whose interests and values it claims to represent (Nilsen 2010: Chapter 8).

Furthermore, this scenario was often coupled with a certain amount of distance between the Andolan's discourse of alternative development and the conceptions of development that preoccupied village activists (see also

Baviskar 1995: Chapters 9 and 10). When I asked village-level activists what they thought 'development' really was or should be, their answers tended to be informed by more immediate concerns of survival: 'Development should be for all; what is this development where some people drown and other people prosper?' 'For us development means that our land should be preserved, we should get enough to eat for the whole year—we don't want anything else'. 'We want development that does not destroy' (interviews, March 2003). Others again would argue that development meant such concrete benefits as having work, access to health care and education, or general material improvements in the standard of living (field notes, March 2003). These statements are arguably expressive of the aspirations of social groups whose most basic needs have been neglected and violated by the dominant direction and meaning of development. Understandably, for them alternative development revolves around basic notions of justice and an emphasis on the necessity of fulfilling basic, material needs and generating tangible improvements in their standards of living.

In important ways, this disjuncture between official discourse and everyday activist understanding of development suggests that movement intellectuals and leaders in the NBA have not managed to develop and translate the ideational apparatus which they have constructed into an idiom which resonates sufficiently with the lived experience of the communities they claim to represent. Nevertheless, much as with the questions raised above about the relevance of movement alliances to subaltern communities, it is important to recognize that this is not an immutable state of affairs. Rather, it is a challenge to be overcome in an as-yet incomplete movement process.

If anything, this challenge underscores the importance of prioritizing dialogical learning and the creation of spaces for such learning as an integral part of the construction of a movement project.

Concluding Remarks

With the completion of the lion's share of the construction work on the SSP in 2006, and the recent resumption of work on the upstream Maheshwar Hydrolectric Project, the Narmada Valley is arguably witnessing the endgame of a process of dispossession and resistance that has spanned two and a half decades. At the heart of this contentious process it is possible to unearth the central fault lines of the political economy of Indian development, namely the pivotal role played by state development strategies in forging structures of proprietary power in such a way as to expand and entrench capitalist relations in postcolonial India. Even though the NBA failed in its struggle to stop the damming of the Narmada River, the trajectory of the Andolan is nevertheless ripe with strategic lessons for the many subaltern movements that are currently emerging as the ever more aggressive neoliberalization of India's economy pries open more spaces to the circuits of capital. Here, I focus on two considerations that I believe to be particularly important.

The trajectory of the NBA yields important lessons about the prospects for fighting dispossession via the institutions, practices, and discourses of the state. As I pointed out in my discussion of the NBA's anti-dam campaign above, the failure of its strategy of jury politics testifies to the fact that its campaign, both directly and indirectly, pushed against and beyond the structural dynamics of India's passive revolution and the role of the state in orchestrating these dynamics. This in turn shows how, in capitalist societies, state power is constituted in such a way as to have 'unequal and asymmetrical effects on the ability of social forces to realize their interests through political action' (Jessop 1982: 224).

This, of course, contrary to the thrust of the arguments made by scholars such as Corbridge and Harriss (2000), constrains the actually existing potential for achieving subaltern empowerment via the institutional ensemble of the state. From this one could draw the conclusion that a political strategy centred on making rights-based claims on the state should be abandoned altogether. Such an argument has been made by Sangeeta Kamat (2002) in her study of social action groups in Adivasi communities in Maharashtra. She argues that state-centred strategies carry the implication that implies that 'politics ... emanates from the state agents as it were, and not from the state structures' (ibid: 124). In short, this strategy entails the internalization among subaltern groups of a 'state idea' which ultimately contributes to the reproduction of the status quo as 'the will towards transformative praxis' is interpreted and mediated in ways that correspond to the liberal democratic mythology of the unbiased state, the result of which is to produce 'consent over the *forms* of political action' (ibid.: 158).

This critique is theoretically cogent, but nonetheless misplaced. In the case of the movement process in the Narmada Valley, its very emergence was predicated on militant particularisms that successfully challenged the everyday tyranny of the local state. In this sense, while it is very much the case that the mobilizing process that unfolded in the dam-affected Adivasi communities in the early and mid-1980s entailed the development of a form of knowledge and skills centred on the principles and procedures of the liberal democratic state, the content of the experience seems to me to be more profoundly related to the realization that overlords could be overthrown and, consequently, that resistance is fertile rather than futile; this is invaluable in a context where state-society relations are as undemocratic as they were in the Adivasi communities in the Narmada Valley.

Seen in this light, jettisoning any engagement with the state would arguably be politically counterproductive for social movements in contemporary India. Rather, the logical strategic conclusion is to argue that activists need to think carefully about which bets to place on the normal political process within an institutionalized social order and which bets to place elsewhere. Strategically, this entails an attempt to steer a course between, on the one hand, anti-statism and, on the other hand, state-centrism. In other words, it entails the advocacy of an *instrumental* rather than a *committed* engagement[11] with the state—that is, an approach to interaction with the institutions, practices, and discourses of the state based on limited expectations of what can be gained and a clear perception of what cannot be gained and what is risked in pursuing this avenue. It also entails an awareness that a challenge to the social structures of power on which the capitalist state rests—if it is to be pursued at all—is a bet best placed on the construction of a social movement project which seeks to develop the collective skilled activity of subaltern groups to the point where it can successfully challenge extant power structures and their entrenched institutional manifestations.

The construction of social movement projects of course comes with challenges, and I believe that a key strategic lesson from the trajectory of the NBA in this respect concerns the limits of oppositional populism. Whereas the adoption of a discourse of resistance centred on oppositional populism is understandable in terms of the strategic constraints involved in the construction of the anti-dam campaign, it is nevertheless problematic in that it restricts the scope of social justice in a way which undermines the emancipatory potential of the social movement project. At a moral level, the failure to address forms of oppression and exploitation within the communities that are mobilized in struggle constitutes a circumscription of the ambit of the project of social justice to the extent that it fails to encompass the situated lifeworlds of the subaltern majorities that ultimately carry a movement project forward.

Overcoming the limits of oppositional populism goes hand in hand with the challenge of achieving a sufficient grounding of social movement projects in the communities that they claim to represent. The successful pursuit of a challenge to a socio-historical totality is ultimately predicated upon the capacity to give direction to the development of the collective skilled activity of subaltern social groups, but such a capacity is unlikely to emerge unless these groups perceive a movement project as relevant to their determinate experiences of domination and their hopes and ambitions for a different future. At the current conjuncture, when the dispossessory ramifications of the neoliberal project in India are engendering a material basis for the construction of alliances between and across campaigns and militant particularisms, it is crucial that the construction of counterhegemonic social movement projects is conducted in a participatory manner, and does not remain the domain of movement elites alone.

Notes

1. A *roti* is a flat, round bread made from stone ground whole meal flour which is a staple in much of central, western and northern India.

2. The construction of Bargi dam led to the flooding of more than 160 villages—far in excess of the 100 or so villages that the state government of Madhya Pradesh had projected as dam-affected—while resettlement and rehabilitation remained a mirage for most of the close to 40,000 oustees (indeed, 26 of the proposed resettlement sites for the Bargioustees were submerged when the floodgates closed in 1990 (see Dharmidhikary n.d.; Schücking 1999; D'Souza 2002).

3. In addition to Bargi, several dams in the project—the Tawa dam (1973), the Barna, Sukta and Kolar dams, and most recently the Indira Sagar Project (2004) and the Sardar Sarovar Project (2006)—have been completed. Other dams—the Maheshwar Hydroelectric Project, the Maan Dam, and the Omkareshwar Dam—are in the process of being built.

4. The term Adivasi literally means "first inhabitant", and was coined by tribal rights activists early in the 20th century to express their claim to being the indigenous people of India. The Indian government does not recognize Adivasis as being indigenous people, but defines Adivasi communities as belonging to the category of Scheduled Tribes as per the Fifth and Sixth Schedules of the Indian Constitution. The Fifth and Sixth Schedules—schedules are lists in the Indian Constitution that categorize and tabulate bureaucratic activity and government policy—provide an array of protective legislation, special entitlements and reservations for Adivasis. See Béteille (1986), Singh (1986), Prasad (2003), Guha (1999), Ratnagar (2003), Bates (1995), Damodaran (2006) and Shah (2007aa) for a selection of perspectives on the issue of indigeneity in the Indian context.

5. NBA slogan.

6. The Narmada Control Authority is a body that was established to monitor and coordinate the activities of the riparian states in relation to the implementation of the SSP.

7. I choose this focus because it was on the national terrain that the outcome of the NBA's campaign was ultimately settled. One of the NBA's great achievements, in addition to putting the issue of displacement squarely at the centre of public debate in India, was of course to campaign successfully at transnational level for the withdrawal of World Bank funding for the SSP. Much has been written about this feature of the Narmada struggle, and I have engaged with this literature in my book (Nilsen 2010: 131-34). However, the fact that the withdrawal of World Bank funding ultimately failed to advance the objective of stopping the construction of the SSP suggests that the major strategic lessons of the movement process in the Narmada Valley can be drawn from the dynamics of contention at the national scale.

8. Yet, curiously for a book published in 2004, Khagram's study makes no mention of the Supreme Court ruling of October 2000. He is content with

establishing that with the turn to the Supreme Court, the SSP conflict 'returned to one of India's critical democratic institutions—the Supreme Court' (Khagram 2004: 135).

9. NBA slogan.
10. In the NBA's repertoire of contention, the term satyagraha is associated with the annual protest events that took place during the monsoon months (June, July, August, September) every year from 1991 onwards until 2002. Basically, what the satyagraha revolved around was a braving of the rising of the waters of the Narmada which set in with the monsoon rains and the closing of the floodgates of the SSP.
11. I owe this distinction to Laurence Cox.

4

Subaltern Resistance in the Bhil Heartland

Historical Trajectories and Contemporary Scenarios

In the late autumn of 2009, a series of unsettling news reports started to call attention to the toll that malnutrition was taking on the Bhil[1] communities of western Madhya Pradesh. In the district of Jhabua, where Adivasis or Scheduled Tribes (STs) constitute 86 per cent of the population, 25 children were reported to have died within the course of only two weeks in the villages of Agasia and Madora, after malnutrition had undermined their immunity levels and rendered them vulnerable to diseases like dengue fever and anaemia (Singh 2009a). By February 2010, the situation had deteriorated even further, as 46 Adivasi children were reported to have died of malnutrition in three villages in the district (Singh 2010a).

The malnutrition deaths in Jhabua in 2009 and 2010 are expressive of the entrenched food insecurity that plagues the state of Madhya Pradesh, where malnutrition rates among children surpass those of most countries in sub-Saharan Africa (Singh 2009b). Indeed, malnutrition takes a particularly harsh toll among the state's Adivasi population, with 71.4 per cent of tribal children in the state being malnourished and 82.5 per cent of tribal children suffering from anaemia. Consequently, whereas the average infant mortality rate (IMR) in the state stands at 70/1000 (compared to a national average of 57/1000), the IMR for ST areas in the state stands at 95.6/1000 (Singh 2010a/b).

Now, the immediate reason for the deaths that occurred in late 2009 and early 2010 can be said to be the failure of public service delivery to the poorest of the poor: human rights activists in Madhya Pradesh pointed out irregularities and shortcomings in the registration of families living below the poverty line in the worst-affected districts, serious flaws in the running of key welfare programmes such as the Public Distribution System (PDS) and the Integrated Child Development Scheme, as well as a severely underdeveloped and underfunded system of public healthcare (Singh 2010a/b). However, there is something more fundamental at play in terms of the causes of child malnutrition deaths than simply governmental neglect. Poverty is the obvious and ultimate reason for widespread food insecurity in the Bhil communities of western Madhya Pradesh, and this poverty is in turn the result of the erosion of Adivasi livelihoods over time. Rainfed subsistence agriculture on land that is increasingly less fertile due to soil erosion is rarely, if ever, sufficient to sustain households through the year. Migrating to the urban centres of Gujarat to find work has consequently become a key survival strategy among the Bhils of western Madhya Pradesh: many Adivasi villages witness 'half of the adult population … absent for half of the year, most working intermittently as casual seasonal labourers in urban construction sites, leaving only the old or the injured; in some villages there will be almost nobody' (Mosse 2007: 16).

Human Development Index—Score and Ranking in Bhil Districts of Madhya Pradesh: 1998-2007[2]

District	*1998*	*2002*	*2007*
Badwani[3]	NA	0.4222 44/45	0.426 44/45
Jhabua	0.356 45/45	0.372 45/45	0.398 45/45
West Nimar	0.401 44/45	0.498 35/45	0.525 33/45
Indore	0.652 1/45	0.694 1/45	0.525 1/45
India	0.451	0.577	0.619

Whereas labour migration has provided some households with access to higher earnings, there is little doubt that the Bhils of western Madhya Pradesh are embedded in a 'political economy of desperation' (Baviskar 2008: 9) that offers few prospects for stable and secure livelihoods. This is perhaps evidenced most clearly in the fact that, between 2007 and 2010, more than 380 Bhil migrant labourers from Jhabua and Alirajpur districts in western Madhya Pradesh had died from silicosis, which they had developed while working in stone quarries in Gujarat (Singh 2011a/b).

Incidence of Poverty in Madhya Pradesh and India, 2004-2005[4]

	Scheduled Tribes (ST)	*Scheduled Castes (SC)*	*Other Backward Castes*	*Other*
Madhya Pradesh Rural	58.6%	42.8%	29.6%	13.4%
Madhya Pradesh Urban	44.7%	67.3%	55.5%	20.8%
India—Rural	47.2%	36.8%	26.7%	16.1%
India—Urban	33.3%	39.9%	31.4%	16.0%

Indeed, the deaths from malnutrition, the dwindling subsistence agriculture, and the increasing resort to labour migration dovetail with both regional and national poverty dynamics among Adivasis. According to official figures, 38 per cent of the population in Madhya Pradesh lived below the poverty line in 2004-5. However, 58.6 per cent of the Scheduled Tribes in the state lived below the poverty line. This fits with findings from the central Indian tribal belt, which stretches from Gujarat and Maharashtra in the west to Jharkhand and Orissa in the east: in the country as a whole, every fourth person lives in poverty, but in the tribal areas of Madhya Pradesh, Gujarat, Rajasthan, Chhattisgarh, Jharkhand and Orissa, two out of every three persons live in poverty. The incidence of chronic poverty among Adivasis is particularly high in Madhya Pradesh and Rajasthan (Sah, Bhatt and Dalapati n.d.: 49-50).

Incidence of Poverty in India by Social Groups—1993-4 and 2004-5[5]

Year	*Rural*			*Urban*		
	SC	*ST*	*All*	*SC*	*ST*	*All*
1993-1994	48.3%	52.0%	37.3%	48.8%	40.1%	32.4%
2004-2005	36.8%	47.7%	28.3%	39.8%	33.9%	25.7%

Furthermore, at the national level, it has been estimated that 44.7 per cent of India's Adivasis lived below the poverty line in 2011; while constituting only 8 per cent of India's total population, they make up as much as 25 per cent of the poorest decile of this population (Mehta, Shepherd, Bhide and Shah 2011; World Bank 2011).[6] In other words, the Adivasis can be rightly described as one of the groups that 'have gained least and lost most from six decades of democracy and development in India' (Guha 2007: 3309).

The poverty suffered by Adivasis in contemporary India is arguably best understood in terms of their 'adverse incorporation' (Hickey and Du Toit 2007) into regional political economies: on this reading, material deprivation is the result of 'the operation of existing social relations and the adverse terms of inclusion in socio-economic systems' (Mosse 2007: 5; see also Mosse 2010). Now, the persistent material deprivations suffered by Adivasi groups like the Bhils of western Madhya Pradesh are further compounded by their disenfranchisement in relation to the state. In western Madhya Pradesh, the immediate cause of disenfranchisement has been the everyday tyranny of the local state. I use the term everyday tyranny to refer to a state-society relation in which villagers encountered the state on a day-to-day basis in the form of petty officials—forest guards, police constables and officers, revenue officials and so on—who imposed a predatory and coercive regime of corruption and violence that effectively denied even the most basic rights and entitlements of Adivasi communities in the region. The corruption and violence of the representatives of the local state articulated with an absence of any kind of substantial awareness of civil liberties, democratic rights, and constitutional provisions among the Bhil communities to produce a culture of fear and deference that effectively reproduced everyday tyranny over time (Nilsen 2010: Chapter 3; see also Baviskar 1995 and chapter 3 in this volume). Against this backdrop, the aim of this chapter is two-pronged: firstly, I shall decipher the historical trajectories through which contemporary patterns of adverse incorporation have crystallized in the region that I refer to as the Bhil heartland (see map below); secondly, I shall present a critical analysis of how collective action by Bhil communities in western Madhya Pradesh has sought to challenge everyday tyranny, and how and how far this mobilization has been successful in democratizing local state-society relations.

The chapter is structured as follows: after a brief discussion of the theoretical orientations that inform my approach to the analysis of state-society relations and subaltern politics in this region, I present a detailed account of the workings of everyday tyranny and locate its genesis in the making of 'colonial state space' (Goswami 2004) in the Bhil heartland during the nineteenth and early twentieth century, and how this process eliminated the relationship of shared sovereignty that had existed between the forest polities of the Bhils and the tributary states of Hindu rulers in the region in the precolonial era, thus subordinating tribal communities to a state whose 'infrastructural power' (Mann 1984) was unprecedented. I then move on to present an analysis of the Adivasi Mukti Sangathan (AMS; Organization for Adivasi Liberation)—a movement that has been active in Badwani and Khargone districts since the early 1990s. Delineating its significant achievements as well as its encounter with brutal forms of state repression, I conclude by discussing why it is necessary to understand local mobilizational trajectories in terms of the contentious crafting of 'big structures and large processes' (Tilly 1984: 11-12) over time in order to make an informed contribution to a key strategic debate for activists in India today: what can social movements hope to achieve by pursuing their oppositional projects in relation to the institutions, discourses, and technologies of rule in and through which state power is embedded, enacted, and exercised?[7]

India and the Bhil Heartland in Madhya Pradesh, Gujarat, Rajasthan and Maharashtra

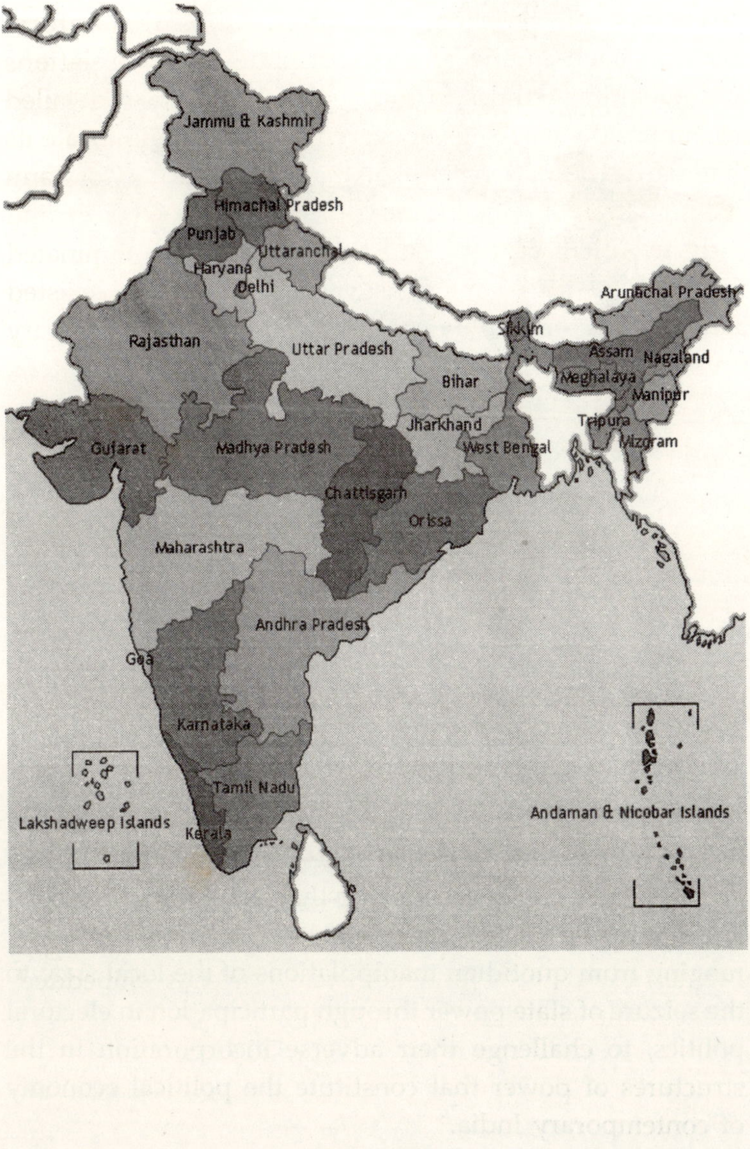

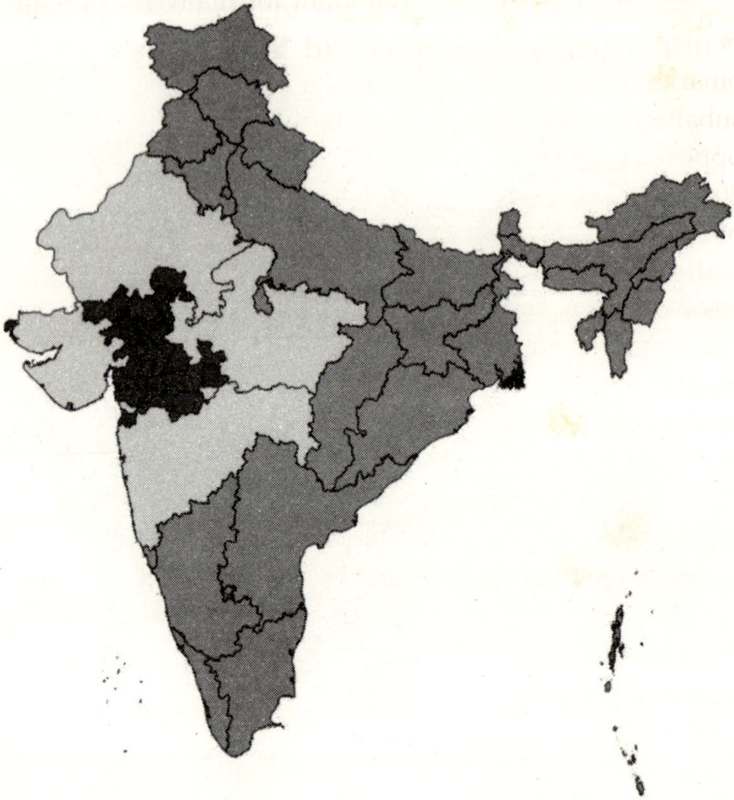

Theoretical Orientations

As I showed in chapter 2, important new ground has been broken in the study of Indian state-society relationships by an emergent body of scholarship that shows how exploited and oppressed groups use the state in a myriad of ways, ranging from quotidian manipulations of the local state to the seizure of state power through participation in electoral politics, to challenge their adverse incorporation in the structures of power that constitute the political economy of contemporary India.[8]

This body of work is important for many reasons, but perhaps most of all because it helps us to move beyond the binaries of the Subaltern Studies project, in which elites and subalterns are thought to inhabit separate and substantially opposed political domains (Guha 1982; see also Chaturvedi 2000b and Ludden 2003). In terms of their understanding of the state, this binary is inscribed in the work of Ranajit Guha (1998, 1999), Partha Chatterjee (1982, 1983a, 1986, 1993) and Sudipta Kaviraj (2010, 2012a/b) in particular. As I showed in detail in chapter 2, their writings portray the modern Indian state as a transmogrification of its colonial predecessor, which has failed to 'create or re-constitute popular common sense around the political world, taking the new conceptual vocabulary of rights, institutions, and impersonal power into the vernacular discourse of rural or small-town Indian society' (Kaviraj 2010: 29). Indeed, even Chatterjee's (2004, 2008) most recent work reproduces the analytical weaknesses of this Manichean view of state-society relations by insisting that while India's elite operates on the terrain of 'civil society' where the liberal precepts of citizenship reign, the country's subaltern groups mobilize in and through 'political society'—that is, the domain of the state which is concerned with the security and welfare of the population. The basic problem with this perspective is, as Subir Sinha (2012: 81) so succinctly puts it, that 'the politics of subalterns have long been transgressive of such divides'. Indeed, the movements of subaltern groups in contemporary India are commonly engaged in struggles that draw on and appropriate existing idioms of citizenship, and in doing so also they arguably also propel the expansion of meanings and practices of citizenship (Agarwala 2008; Subramanian 2009; Sundar 2011; Gudavarthy 2012).

A key virtue of the new wave of work on state-society relations is that it has proven capable of engaging analytically with the complex and composite dynamics that characterize actually-existing subaltern politics in India today.[9] It is notable that many of the key contributions to this literature draw on a Foucauldian understanding of power relations and state power.[10] Above all, Foucault's notion of governmentality is put to use to understand how state-sponsored programmes geared towards improving the welfare and enabling the empowerment of poorer groups provide interstitial spaces where 'new kinds of resistances' can take place (Gupta 2001: 66). Key to this argument is the assertion that the state should not be conceptualized as 'a unitary centre of power' but rather in terms of 'multiple and contradictory articulations of power that emanate from no fixed axis' (Williams, Vira and Chopra 2011: 17). And precisely for this reason, the state is riddled with 'fissures and ruptures' that enable subaltern groups 'to create possibilities for political action and activism' (Gupta 1995: 394).

By enabling a shift of conceptual orientation away from the assumed existence of 'hermetically sealed sites of autonomy' towards an understanding of 'relational spaces of connection and articulation' (Moore 1998: 347) in the study of subaltern politics, this body of work has clearly been of singular importance. However, as I have argued at length elsewhere, there is a serious lacuna in this body of work, which is ultimately rooted in its theoretical underpinnings (see also Nilsen, 2011, 2012a/b and chapter 2 in this volume). The Foucauldian emphasis on the decentred nature of power comes with the limitation of not being able to properly address the questions of how and why, at specific and contingent conjunctures, the exercise of state power achieves a certain unity across dispersed sites, and the limits that this may impose upon the prospects for advancing subaltern agency in relation to the state. In order to address this shortcoming, I believe it is necessary to develop a historical-sociological approach which is capable of conceptualizing how the micro-politics of state-society relations and the political economy of capitalist development and state formation as 'master change processes' (Tilly 1982) are mutually constitutive, and how this relationship ultimately circumscribes the scope for pursuing subaltern resistance via the institutional and discursive apparatuses of the state. I presented a full account of what such a perspective might look like in chapter 2 above, so here I will restrict myself to an outline of its most basic tenets.

The first and most basic point is to think of subalternity not as 'an essential characteristic of being' (Moore 1998: 352) but as a determinate positionality within what E.P. Thompson (1978: 151) would call 'a societal "field-of-force"'. A societal field of force is in turn best understood as the outcome of those processes through which 'the hegemony of a fundamental social group over a series of subordinate groups' (Gramsci 1998: 182) is constituted. Constructing hegemony entails gaining the consent of subaltern groups to 'the general direction' (ibid.: 12) that dominant groups seek to impose on social life. Consequently, the result is 'a continuous process of formation and superseding of unstable equilibria ... between the interests of the fundamental group and those of the subordinate groups' (ibid.: 182).

The negotiated character of hegemony has ramifications for how we understand the positionality and agency of subaltern groups. In terms of positionality, the central point is that subaltern groups are embedded in socioeconomic relations, political institutions, and cultural forms that—despite concessions and compromises—buttress the reproduction of hegemony. The logical corollary of this is that subaltern agency will tend to proceed through contentious appropriations of what Adam Morton (2007: 92) has called 'the social condensations of hegemony'—that is, through hegemonic political institutions, discourses and processes, rather than at a distance from these (Gramsci 1998: 52-55; Green 2002). The limitations and constrictions inherent to this experience may propel groups to develop forms of self-organization that are better suited to advance their interests. And crucially, autonomy, rather than being an intrinsic feature of subalternity, is an achievement—the outcome of struggle that ruptures hegemony and thus drives 'the line of development towards integral autonomy' (Gramsci 1998: 52).

Gramsci (1998: 260) noted that, in contrast to the ruling groups of previous eras, dominant groups under capitalism seek 'to construct an organic passage from the other classes into their own'. The state plays a pivotal role in this process through institutions, discourses and technologies of rule that bring about 'an increasingly more sophisticated internal articulation and condensation of social relations within a given state form' (Thomas 2009: 140). There are two points that should be noted in extending this argument to the dynamics of subaltern politics.

Firstly, it is precisely because of the construction of organic passages between dominant and subaltern groups that state formation as a master change process comes to articulate with the 'local rationalities' (Cox 1999; Nilsen 2009; Nilsen and Cox 2013) that animate subaltern politics. As Corrigan and Sayer (1985: 4) point out, state formation is predicated on forms of 'moral regulation' that seek to regulate social life by propagating idioms that seek to give 'unitary and unifying expression' to inherently variegated experiences of social life. But when there is a dissonance between the 'universalizing vocabularies' (ibid.: 7) that are at the heart of bourgeois state formation and the lived experiences of subaltern groups, these vocabularies can easily become 'sites of protracted struggle as to what they mean and for whom' (ibid.: 6) as subaltern groups mobilize to contest their adverse incorporation in a given social formation.

Secondly, because the state is congealed from social relations characterized by a 'compromise equilibrium' (Gramsci 1998: 161) between dominant and subaltern groups, there will also be 'conjunctural opportunities' (Jessop 1982: 225) for such contestation to advance via the modalities of state power. However, the compromises that have been struck are always ones 'in which the interests of dominant groups prevail' (Gramsci 1998: 182). This in turn means that conjunctural opportunities exist in dialectical tension with 'structural constraints' (Jessop 1982: 225)—the state, in other words, 'is an ensemble of power centres that offer unequal chances to different forces within and outside the system to act for different political purposes' (Jessop 2008: 37).

The challenge facing a historical-sociological approach to the study of subaltern politics is thus to trace the links between a specific set of state-society relations and the conflictual unfolding of capitalist development and state formation as master change processes in order to analyse the achievements and limitations of particular trajectories of mobilization. In the next two parts of this chapter I do this by first analysing the anatomy of everyday tyranny and tracing its historical lineage to colonial state-making projects in the Bhil heartland of western India and then detailing the rise and fall of one specific movement—the Adivasi Mukti Sangathan—as it sought to democratize local state-society relations.

Everyday Tyranny and the Making of Colonial State Space

The Anatomy of Everyday Tyranny

'We people who live in the forest aren't as frightened of the lion as we are of the people who wear pants', said Govindbhai,[11] a Bhil activist from Badwani district, as he tried to explain how the Adivasi communities in the region had lived in fear of the local state and its officials:

> We felt that we would always walk with our eyes low on the ground. Those who are city-dwellers or police, *patwari*[12] and *thanedars*,[13] all the time they are like parasites, sucking on us, always demanding *ghee*,[14] chickens and money. Whatever they wanted, they took away from us—grains, *mirch*,[15] and *daal*.[16] What could we do? (Interview, February 2010).

Govindbhai's account encapsulates many of the key facets of everyday tyranny as a state-society relationship. The Bhil communities in western Madhya Pradesh would encounter the state through petty officials such as forest guards, police, and *patwaris* who on various pretexts would demand bribes in cash and kind from the villagers. These exactions were underpinned by the threat and actual use of force; refusing the demands of a police officer or a forest guard would result in a savage beating at the hands of the officials. The local state and its officials inspired fear and deference among the Bhils and thus denied even the most basic rights and entitlements of Adivasi communities in the region.

A key hinge in the machinations of everyday tyranny in the region has been the clash between, on the one hand, Adivasi use of the forest for cultivation, grazing, and as a source of timber for construction, wood for fuel, and minor forest produce for market exchange, and, on the other, the state's ownership of and control over forests. For example, for Bhil communities in western Madhya Pradesh, clearing forestland and using it for cultivation—a practice known as *nevad*—is an integral survival strategy. However, when they engage in this practice, Adivasis are effectively in breach of forest laws that posit the state as the exclusive owner of forests in India and which categorize *nevad* and other uses of the forest for livelihood and survival as "encroachments" on state property (Gadgil and Guha 1993; Prasad 2004).

The fact that the customary practices of local communities were in fact illegal in turn came to serve as a lever for corrupt and coercive exactions by the forest guards that patrolled the Bhil habitats. Suraj,[17] an activist with the Adivasi Mukti Sangathan, gave the following account of the corruption of the forest guards in Badwani and Khargone districts:

> The Adivasis are nothing without the forest. The Adivasis' work is never complete without going to the jungle. If we want to make *rotis*, we need wood but we have to pay to bring that wood from the forest ... Sometimes, in the wind and the rain, if our huts fall down and we need wood to repair them, even for that we would have to pay. If we want to make a hut with one small room, then we have to pay them 1000 rupees. If we want to

> make a hut with two or three small rooms, then the person who makes this has to pay at least 5000 rupees. And only then would they let them make this hut. Otherwise they would beat the person and torture him. (Interview, November 2009).

Suraj proceeded to explain how the forest guards would extort bribes on a regular basis from the villages: 'The forest-*wallahs* would take *chanda* as and when it pleased them. Chicken, *ghee*—they would just take it from our homes as and when they wished. Even for doing *kheti*, they would take *chanda*.' The word *chanda* actually means donation, but is used here to refer to the fact that forest guards would claim money, chicken, ghee and other assets as something that the villagers owed to them due to their position in the state hierarchy. In fact, in some villages, providing *chanda* to the forest guards in order to be able to use the forests had become so regularized that the *patels*—the village headmen—would approach the local forest department outposts carrying "donations" on behalf of an entire village. Serving also as the conduit through which the state extended its reach into village communities, the *patels* would pocket a share of the money collected from the village, and were thus coopted into the workings of everyday tyranny (interview, Rameshbhai,[18] March 2010; field notes, February 2003).

In Alirajpur district, just north of Badwani, activists would tell stories about how, if the forest guards found villagers walking along the road carrying a sickle, they would accuse them of going to collect fodder and beat them up; without fail, the officials would demand bribes in exchange for dropping criminal charges. Similarly, if people were caught carrying an axe or a load of firewood, they would be on the receiving end of beatings and extortion (field notes, February 2003). Claiming to intervene in the name of law and order, local police would crack down on the illegal distillation of *mahua* liquor in Bhil homes or disputes between households in the villages and, like the forest guards, demand bribes in money or in kind in order to turn a blind eye to the offence (field notes, 2003, 2009-2010). Thus Suraj reflected: 'Earlier on, the police and forest-*wallahs* had total command over this area' (interview, November 2009).

This command was reproduced over time, as the absence of an awareness of the basic rights of citizenship combined with a knowledge of the harm that state officials could inflict to produce a culture of fear and deference. A group of activists from a village in Khargone district portrayed local perceptions of state officials as follows:

> They didn't know and whenever any authority came to their house; they thought that God himself had come. They were very afraid and whenever someone came, they would get even more frightened and start to tremble with fear. If the forest or police-*wallahs* came, then along with the children, even the elders would disappear into their houses. At that time, the looting was extreme and whatever was asked for had to be given to these people. We didn't know anything about any laws or rules. The *patel* only would communicate with the *sarkar*, the forest guards and the police, and everyone was scared to interfere with what the *patel* said. They were afraid that if they did interfere, they wouldn't be allowed to live in the village any more. If we went to the *thana*, the police would say: "Why have you come here? Are you the *patel*? Go back and come with your *patel*." They would say like this (Group interview, February 2010).

Dediya,[19] a prominent activist from Alirajpur district, argued that the everyday tyranny of the state and its officials had come to be entrenched as a tradition in the area—the blatant illegalities of forest guards and police were assumed to act in accordance with what was their right: 'People, well, they had seen this happen for a long time, even before independence ... so there was always a fear of the state, from rule in that sense.' He went on to explain how this culture of fear and deference had become sedimented as tradition: '[Local people] just thought these must be the rules—that there must be some rule about chickens, to beat must have been a law—because these *thanedars*, police, they represented the law and they were always beating people up, so that must have been the law, so they thought. Many people assumed these were the laws, accepted them, and it became tradition' (interview, April 2010).

Thus, in western Madhya Pradesh, the everyday tyranny of local officials had been woven into the fabric of daily life to such an extent that it had become a guiding principle of how relations and interactions between Adivasis and the state were supposed to be structured (see also Baviskar 1995). There may well have been discontent with the rapaciousness of state officials—indeed, it is hard to believe that there wasn't, given the persistent brutality and condescension meted out—but a 'public transcript' (Scott 1990) of deference and obedience was adopted as a survival strategy in the Bhil communities of western Madhya Pradesh. Acquiescence in the face of a seemingly all-powerful state whose workings are at best opaque is of course entirely understandable when considered in terms of the compulsions of marginality[20]—the necessity of securing a livelihood leaves little scope for anything but the path of least resistance, especially when considering the severe punishment that defiance of any kind is likely to provoke. Simultaneously, there can be no doubt that the public transcript of deference and obedience also contributed to cementing the adverse incorporation of Adivasis in the regional political economy. In the next section, I develop a historical analysis that may go some way towards explaining the deep-rooted nature of subordination and deference in the Bhil heartland.

Making Colonial State Space in the Bhil Heartland

The current scenario of poverty and disenfranchisement in western Madhya Pradesh is rooted in the transformation of the political economy of the Bhil heartland that started unfolding in the wake of the British defeat of the Marathas in 1818 and as a result of the consolidation of colonial power in western India. There is of course no space here to discuss in detail the relationships that existed between Bhils, Rajputs, and Marathas in western India during the precolonial era.[21] However, what must be established is that a narrative in which the Bhils are portrayed as autochthons defining themselves in opposition to the tributary states of Rajput and Maratha rulers is deeply problematic. Constituted on the basis of what Eric Wolf (1982) called 'kin-ordered' modes of production, Bhil chiefdoms 'were in fact deeply integrated into the political economy of medieval India' (Guha 1999: 121).

Ajay Skaria (1999) has called attention to how this integration was expressed in the fact that Bhil chieftains would claim dues known as *haks* or *giras haks* from the peasant villages in the plains, which would be claimed through raids if they were withheld. Crucially, Rajput and Maratha rulers recognized these claims as legitimate, and interpreted raids as an indication that it would be necessary to renegotiate Bhil claims on the villages within their realm. In this sense, then, the relationship between Bhil forest polities and Hindu tributary states were mediated through the construction of 'shared sovereignty' (Skaria 1998: 208).

Now, shared sovereignty can arguably be understood as a foundational principle for the structuring of political power in tributary states. Given that tributary states were congealed from a mode of surplus appropriation in which monarchical rulers depended on a complex lattice-work of relations with aristocratic fief-holders and landowners, they were of course also faced with what John Haldon (1993: 156) refers to as 'the tributary constraint'—that is, the challenge posed by the countervailing and centripetal forces constituted by the ruling elite that actually appropriates surplus from the peasantry (see also Banaji 2010: 18-26). In this context, governing does not so much centre on the territorial extension of sovereignty outwards from a singular and central point of authority within a clearly defined territorial space, but rather hinges on attempts to 'manage the ebb and flow of this internal tension that was part and parcel of the historical dynamics of all traditional agrarian, subject-peasant ... societies' (Berktay 1991: 260). The recognition of Bhil *haks*, the acknowledgement of the authority of Bhil chieftains, and the negotiations of claims in the wake of raids—these are arguably best understood as a set of manifestations of one particular way of managing this ebb and flow of internal tensions. What the coming of the Raj entailed, then, was not so much the constitution of a relationship between tribal autochthons and a state-making project where before there had been none; rather, the crafting of colonial state space changed the terms of Bhil integration into the regional political economy of western India.

The term 'colonial state space' has been coined by Manu Goswami (2004: 8) to refer to 'a spectacular reworking' of the colonial state in the transition from a 'mercantile colonialism' to 'territorial colonialism' in the wake of the Great Uprising of 1857. Whereas mercantile colonialism under the aegis of the East India Company was centred on 'the extraction of tribute and the expansion of trade', 'territorial colonialism' under the British Crown conceived of the colonies as 'substantially and functionally internal supplements of a globe-spanning and hierarchically configured imperial space economy' (ibid.: 45, 44). In this process, Goswami argues, the socioeconomic geography of colonial India was transformed, the modalities of state power were consolidated, and the reach of state-generated classificatory schemes was deepened (ibid.: 9).

Now, in the Bhil heartland, the making of colonial state space can arguably be said to date as far back as the second quarter of the nineteenth century, and it is my contention that it is also in these interventions that we can locate the origins of contemporary forms of adverse incorporation in the region. In terms of the economic geography of the region, concerted efforts were made by the British to encourage the Bhils, whose livelihoods had been centred on shifting cultivation, to settle down as 'quiet and obedient cultivators' (Graham 1856: 219) whose taxes would add to the coffers of the Bombay Presidency. Perhaps even more importantly, from the middle of the nineteenth century onwards, the colonial state claimed ownership and control over forest areas that were integral to the Bhil livelihood through legislation that enabled 'the enclosure of large areas of landscape as reserved forests' that were inaccessible to the Bhils (Whitehead 2012: 15).[22] Sedentarization failed to transform the Bhils into a prosperous, tax-paying peasantry. Yielding instead an extreme dependency on usurious moneylenders and in some cases widespread land alienation, this policy combined with forest enclosures to give rise to the marginal subsistence peasant who today scrambles for survival in western India's informal economy (Guha 1999).

However, if we want to understand the making of everyday tyranny as a state-society relationship, it is necessary to investigate how the consolidation of the modalities of state power unfolded in the Bhil heartland in such a way as to eliminate shared sovereignty and subordinate Bhil communities to a state whose infrastructural power had been vastly augmented by comparison with precolonial tributary states.

The colonial state, Goswami (2004: 31) argues, was unswerving in its commitment 'to spreading its authority evenly throughout the territory'. In the Bhil heartland, this process started with the military pacification of Khandesh in eastern Maharashtra in the 1820s, which became particularly effective after the formation of the Khandesh Bhil Corps (KBC; a military outfit of Bhil recruits, headed by a British officer) in 1825 (Simcox 1912; Outram 1853; Guha 1999). Military pacification was followed by the settlement of former insurgents as peasant cultivators. A pardon was offered on condition that the Bhils not challenge British authority in the future; the *haks* of the Bhil chieftains were investigated and settled, and, in order to bring an end to raiding, paid as 'colonial pensions' (Guha 1999: 141).

In the Dangs in eastern Gujarat, this process was set in train in 1830, when the KBC carried out a three-month campaign in order to bring an end to Dangi raids on the Khandesh plains. The process that followed, in which the chiefs' claims to *giras haks* were settled by the colonial state, illustrates the centrality of the extirpation of shared sovereignty in the construction of colonial state space. As in Khandesh some years before, the key transformation was that *giras haks* now came to be paid to the Dangi chiefs from the coffers of the Khandesh treasury. As Skaria (1999: 162) points out, this is highly significant: it alters the meaning of *haks* altogether as they come to be a 'conferral from above' rather than a rightful claim infused with meanings of sovereignty and power.

Similar processes unfolded in other parts of the Bhil heartland. In Mewar in southern Rajasthan this assumed the form of a protracted conflict between the Anglo-Sisodia regime and the Bhil chieftains of Bhomat and Magra over the chieftains' rights to levy taxes on merchants and travellers on the Udaipur-Ahmedabad road (Mathur 1988; Singh 1995; Sen 2005a/b). Although eventually recognized as legitimate by both the British and the Mewar court, the material and symbolic substance of these taxes had been eroded by the late nineteenth century (Sen 2005a/b).

In western Madhya Pradesh, military pacification occurred in the 1820s and 1830s. By the 1840s, a more conciliatory line developed, centred on the settlement of Bhil claims to dues into pensions payable from the princely courts of states like Alirajpur and Badwani. However, there was little incentive for the Rajput courts to comply with the agreements that had been negotiated, given that raids were now subject to military retaliation by the colonial state (Kela 2012: 138). By the late nineteenth century, pacification and settlement had created a situation in which the ruling elites of states like Badwani and Alirajpur 'possessed almost uncontested authority over [their] "kingdom"... These developments increasingly led small kings to dissociate themselves from the now relatively powerless forest polities' (Skaria 1999: 174).

Pacification and settlement was followed by concerted efforts to develop the 'infrastructural power' (Mann 1984) of the state in relation to its Bhil subjects. In a state like Alirajpur this is particularly evident in a striving to expand and consolidate fiscal capacities. The initial attempts in this direction can be traced as far back as 1869, when Alirajpur came under British superintendence. At this point in time, the Bhil Agent 'found the treasury empty, and this was said to be its chronic state' (AAR 1869: 1). Thus a series of fiscal reforms were introduced to increase revenue from land, forests and excise (see Kela 2012: 205-6). A new phase in this process was set in train from the second decade of the twentieth century onwards; once again it was land and forest revenue, along with excise duties, that were the key foci of reform. In all three domains, there is a relatively clear tendency towards increased revenue flows, reflected in the overall revenue levels of Alirajpur state, which display a relatively steady process of improvement from 1910-11 to 1939-40.

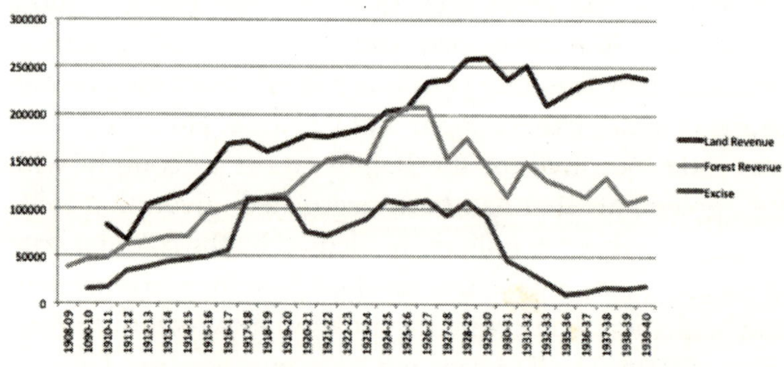

Chart 4.1: Revenue Flows, Alirajpur State, 1908-1940 (Compiled from Alirajpur Administrative Reports 1910-11 to 1939-40)

The increases in fiscal capacity that clearly took place in the Rajput royal houses of western Madhya Pradesh in the early twentieth century are of course significant as indicators of the increased infrastructural power of the princely states, and therefore of the ability of these states to exercise their authority in relation to Bhil communities in a far more unequivocal way than before. However, this is also an important development in that it brings into being the ensemble of coercive institutions through which everyday tyranny is enacted.

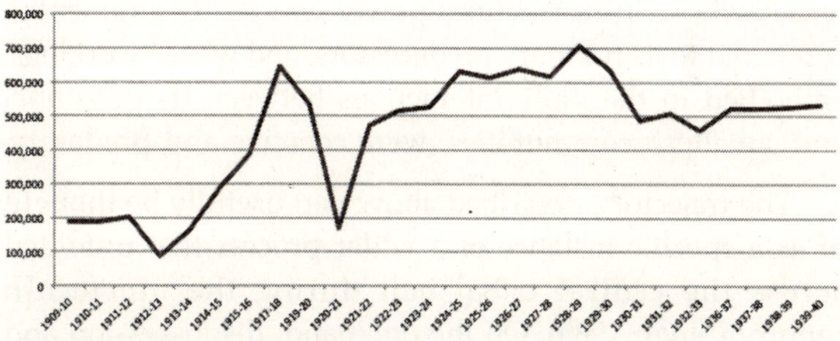

Chart 4.2: State Revenue, Alirajpur, 1909-1940
(Compiled from Alirajpur Administrative
Reports 1909-10 to 1939-40)

This was the case not just in western Madhya Pradesh area, but throughout the Bhil heartland. It is perhaps best illustrated by the nefarious role the Forest Department came to play in everyday life in Bhil communities throughout western India. Alongside the police and the *patwaris*, forest guards soon became 'the new kings of the forest' in the Bhil heartland (Guha 1999: 160). Indeed, the complaints recorded in Thana district in the late nineteenth century are almost identical to the contemporary narratives of Bhil Adivasis discussed above: 'If the (forest) guard meets us he ill-treats us. He makes us give him fowls for nothing, when we cut wood for our houses'. Testifying even further to the extent to which the everyday tyranny of the forest guards had been woven into the fabric of social life in Bhil communities, a colonial official in 1938 wrote that in west Khandesh 'instances of assault, beatings, and hurt are of such constant occurrence that they do not arouse much comment locally, unless unusual brutality has occurred' (ibid.: 170). Thus, a new state-society relation was forged in the Bhil heartland from 1818 onwards in which Bhil communities were adversely incorporated as the subordinates of a state apparatus whose sovereignty was constructed in singular terms, whose infrastructural power was vastly augmented compared to its tributary predecessors, and whose workings, embodied in the daily interactions between its personnel and subaltern communities, were coercive and predatory.

The trajectory described above can usefully be thought of as a specific instance of a wider process that unfolded across the central tribal belt during the nineteenth century (Singh 1985). On the one hand, dispossession and subordination created the marginal subsistence peasant who was subject to the depredations of a state dominated by regional elites. On the other hand, the confluence of colonial anthropology and anthropometry, legal palliatives devised to counter land alienation and usury, and the crafting of technologies of rule from the Scheduled Districts Act of 1874, gave rise to the concept of the tribal as a colonial subject in need of protection (Bates 1995a/b; Guha 1999: Chapter 2; Shah 2007a). The result, ultimately, was the genesis, both materially and symbolically, of the 'tribal slot' (Li 1999) in India's political economy. This slot would in turn be appropriated and inverted from the 1920s onwards, as activists in Chota Nagpur developed the concept of the Adivasi as an insurgent collective identity which made claims on the state for recognition and redistribution in order to remedy the injustices wrought by the 'colonial transformation of tribal society in middle India' (Singh 1978).[23] As I show in the next section of the chapter, this would also shape the shape and form of Bhil mobilization in western Madhya Pradesh in the 1990s.

Democratic Struggles in the Bhil Heartland Today

Preliminaries

My narrative of the crafting of colonial state space in the Bhil heartland during what can be called the long nineteenth century from 1818 to the 1940s has deliberately made little reference to Bhil resistance to the changes that were brought about in this period. I have done this in order to be able to weave together a series of complex changes across an internally variegated region into a sufficiently brief and clear analytical narrative. It should be noted, however, that the period in question was also a 'rebellious century' (Tilly, Tilly and Tilly 1975) in which Bhil communities across the heartland were engaged in what might be called contentious negotiations with the state-making projects of princely rulers and colonial authorities in a number of ways, ranging from petitioning to large-scale uprisings.

However, in western Madhya Pradesh as in much of the rest of the Bhil heartland, the state-society relationship that was crafted under the aegis of colonial rule was reproduced after independence. In western Madhya Pradesh, this was a result of the way in which the Congress Party integrated former princely rulers into its ranks as the commanders of key vote banks (Jaffrelot 2008). Consequently, the same princely rulers who had been able to extricate themselves from relations of shared sovereignty with the Bhil forest polities through their engagement with colonial state-making strategies, could now reproduce their hegemonic position through their integration into the 'dominant party system' (Corbridge and Harriss 2000: 53) that emerged in India after 1947.

When sustained mobilization from below against the everyday tyranny started to crystallize in Alirajpur and Khargone districts in the 1980s, this was connected to a wider phase of resistance that had begun in the Bhil heartland in the early 1970s. The dispossession and subordination of Bhils and other Adivasi groups in northeastern Maharashtra came to be vigorously contested from 1973 onwards by several local social movements in Dhulia and Thane districts.[24] This process spilled over into western Madhya Pradesh in the early 1980s, when the Khedut Mazdoor Chetna Sangath (KMCS) emerged in Alirajpur, which at this point in time was a *tehsil* of Jhabua district.[25] During the 1990s, several other local movements emerged: the Adivasi Mukti Sangathan in Khargone district, the Adivasi Shakti Sangathan/Adivasi Morcha Sangathan in Dewas district, the Jagrit Adivasi Dalit Sangathan in Badwani district, and the Shramik Adivasi Sangathan in Betul and Harda districts.

The achievements of these movements in terms of curbing the excesses of a notoriously high-handed state have been substantial. However, in this arc of resistance it is also possible to discern another salient feature, namely the deployment of state coercion against these movements. In the rest of this section, I present a detailed analysis of the trajectory of one of these movements, the Adivasi Mukti Sangathan (AMS), and discuss its implications in terms of thinking strategically about subalterns and the state in contemporary India.

Breaking the Spell of Everyday Tyranny

In Khargone district,[26] a challenge was mounted to everyday tyranny in the early 1990s, when two middle-class activists who had honed their craft with the Communist Party of India arrived in the town of Sendhwa to start organizing among the Bhil communities in the district. What stood out to the two activists as they started to become more familiar with the region was the way in which the Bhils were subject to the coercive extortions of what one of them, Bijoybhai,[27] appropriately referred to as an 'unholy nexus' of forest guards, police, patwaris, and moneylenders, and that the dominance of this nexus was secured by the fear that it inspired: '[W]e underlined the most critical problem as the fear factor amongst the natives of this area. That is they were exploited, suppressed, brutally killed. And even if they were cheated, they were not able to open their voice. They were really voiceless'. This realization in turn fed into the way in which they decided to pursue mobilization in the Bhil communities: 'So our initial strategy was to create a situation where people can have their own voice before anything. So that was the motive behind the organization' (interview, November 2009).

In order to work towards this, the two activists initially drew on pre-existing contacts in the region to call meetings with villagers where they would discuss the problems that the Adivasi communities experienced in their relationship with the state and its officials, as well as with moneylenders and merchants who ruled supreme in the region's market-towns. In order to prove that resistance to the everyday tyranny of the state was not simply futile, a trip was organized across the state border, to Thane district in Maharashtra, to enable interaction with Adivasi activists there. Following this initial exposure to the fact that 'these small little people could put up a very big challenge to all those exploiters', a new round of discussions was organized, and it was decided that a direct action should be organized to challenge local authorities on their neglect of schools and the lacking provision of drinking water in the district (interview, November 2009).

According to Bijoybhai, there was a strategic rationale to this decision. Firstly, making state authorities and their neglect of Bhil communities the first target and issue of mobilization would hopefully contribute to forging a collective identity, as it would be easy to draw a line between a clear-cut 'us' (the poor Adivasis) and an equally clear-cut 'them' (the powerful *sarkar*). Secondly, it was hoped that it would be relatively easy to secure a victory, or at least a substantial concession on the issues of water and education, compared, for example, to issues such as forest rights or usurious moneylending: '[T]he first struggle needs to be won, not to be lost. If we lose then the inspiration and commitment ... do not get crystallized' (interview, November 2009). A survey of some 26 villages was carried out, demonstrating that schools were not being run properly and that even in a drought year water was not being provided in the villages. Then, in early May 1992, a rally was organized in front of the *tehsil* offices in Sendhwa, which attracted as many as 5,000 people, many of whom were women. Fiery speeches were given against the authorities' neglect of education and water-facilities in the villages, and the women who had brought along clay pots that would normally be used for storing water smashed these on the staircase of the tehsil office. In response, the *tehsildar*, who was otherwise a man who inspired fear among the Bhil communities in the region, assured the demonstrators that he would address their complaints promptly (interview, November 2009).

From Bijoybhai's perspective, the main point about this agitation was 'that people should voice [their grievances] before the authority. We succeeded!' (interview, November 2009). Indeed, the concrete act of addressing state officials assertively in connection with grievances and issues figures prominently in the narratives of Bhil activists as an experience of speaking truth to power that was crucial in rupturing their fear of these officials and the apparatus they represented: 'In the beginning, when I started to muster up the courage to speak to the police, thanedar, patwaris—then my fears began to go away', explained one activist (interview, February 2010). However, in addition to this, claims-making on the state also yielded tangible results that helped the mobilization to gain momentum. Bamniya,[28] one of the most seasoned Bhil activists in the AMS, explained the changes that occurred as follows:

> Slowly, wherever there was no access to good drinking water, [the *tehsildar*] immediately made arrangements for water on bullock carts, and where hand pumps were possible, they were dug. Wherever there were schools without teachers, arrangements for teachers were made, wherever nurses weren't there, they were sent. It was like this in the beginning ... and if it wasn't coming then we would complain again, and so slowly things like this started happening routinely.

The outcome was that 'people's work was getting done, so people thought there was strength in the Sangathan, and the *sarkar*, the *sarkari* workers, they [became] afraid of the Sangathan'. And 'at that point', Bamniya argued, 'people thought: "No, bhai, there is strength in the Sangathan and when it fights, there are results, it works." For this reason the Sangathan spread in the whole region' (interview, November 2009).

This was only one of many similar actions and campaigns that the AMS pursued as it built itself up over the next few years. Gradually, the Sangathan took on the malpractices of the *patwaris*, police corruption and brutality, the corrupt exactions of the forest guards, land alienation at the hands of moneylenders, and also the criminal business networks of the liquor mafia in the district. What is arguably most significant about this early stage of the mobilizing process is that it effectively broke the spell of everyday tyranny in the Adivasi communities in the district: active participation in mobilization, and the concessions and victories won through militant actions, served as an experiential counterweight to the received wisdom that the local state and its officials were all-powerful and invincible overlords that could not and should not be challenged in any way. With these new experiences, emotional dispositions changed: 'What should I be afraid of?' a woman activist asked rhetorically. 'Because of roaming [with the Sangathan] every day, the fear has left me. I have even gone to jail and back and I'm not even afraid of the jail!' (interview, November 2009). Slowly but surely the state started to appear less as an entity that was to be feared and obeyed and more as an institution that it was possible to defy, to challenge, and to make claims on.

Creating a Vernacular Rights Culture

'Everybody would say and think that the *sarkar* is the biggest among us', reflected Govindbhai when asked to explain how villagers perceived the state prior to the coming of the Sangathan. 'They thought that the hands of the *sarkar* were very big. Whatever the authorities say, that must be done. The village had no status at all'. But this changed as mobilization got underway:

> They would say that the *sarkar's* arm is big and long. It was later on that we realized that, in reality, the *sarkar's* arm is long because we are the ones who have voted and made the *sarkar*—then we should also know what the law is, right? Later on we realized that they are making fools of us, so how is the *sarkar's* arm long? (interview, February 2010).

Govindbhai's reflections are significant, because they point towards a fundamental transformation in the way that the state is perceived. Crucially, the state went from being viewed and understood as an external agency that could impose its power upon the village community at will to being seen as an institution that in fact derived its powers—its very being, in fact—from people acting as citizens. This, of course, is a major reversal of the grammar of everyday tyranny, and it is a change that testifies to the substantially democratizing impact that the activism of the AMS had on state-society relations—an impact that in crucial ways was driven by the awareness of rights and the familiarity with bureaucratic procedures that the movement fostered among its activists. For example, Barlibai,[29] a leading female activist with the Sangathan, emphasized how she had learned 'the way in which to talk, how to talk to officers and authorities, how to get the work done, this knowledge I have got. I got this learning.' (interview, March 2010). Speaking about how the forest guards in the area had earlier extracted bribes unopposed, Suraj argued that '[w]hen the Sangathan came into being, then the realization came that this was all wrong and the awareness of our rights was generated. We should not give money and chickens. In the government, the functionaries are the servants of the public' (interview, November 2009).

One of the central themes in activist accounts of their participation in the mobilization process was the collective learning that flowed from it: activists would typically talk about how they had acquired knowledge about basic democratic rights and citizenship, about the constitutional entitlements of Scheduled Tribes, and about how the machinery of the state is supposed to work and how to relate to its procedures and practices. This process can perhaps usefully be contrasted to what Alpa Shah (2007b, 2010) has found to be the prevailing response to elite domination of the local state among Munda Adivasis in Jharkhand: rather than 'keeping the state away' through disengagement and a turn towards a traditional sacral polity beyond the power of the local elites and the secular Indian state, the activism of the AMS changed the terms upon which the state was present in the everyday lives of Bhil communities. Thus, if the transformation of emotional dispositions that I discussed above made the state less fearsome in the eyes of the Bhil communities, collective learning about rights, entitlements and bureaucratic procedures also made it a much less opaque entity than it had previously been. The combined effect of these changes was to draw in the reins of the state in its everyday workings, and to make it markedly more accountable to subaltern groups who 'seek to engage with the state as citizens, or as members of populations with legally defined rights or politically inspired expectations' (Corbridge, Williams, Srivastava, and Véron 2005: 13).

However, it would be problematic to consider this simply as the implementation or unfolding of a universal democratic script at the local level. As Ajantha Subramanian

(2003: 135) has argued, democratic struggles from below also entail 'reworking state categories' to inflect them with meanings that are expressive of the situated needs and desires of subaltern groups. Therefore, it may also be more appropriate to conceive of the democratizing impact of the Sangathan's struggles in terms of what Madhok (2010) calls 'vernacular rights cultures'—a term which derives its relevance from the acknowledgement that rights cultures cannot simply be reduced to or understood in terms of the standard political and normative vocabulary of liberal democracy. Instead, vernacular rights cultures emerge from and are refracted through 'regional histories of claims making' (Subramanian 2009: 3) and are consequently also inflected with particular vernacular idioms (Michelutti 2008). In the case of the politics of the AMS, this became manifest in the way in which activists would conceive of themselves as right-bearers not so much in terms of the universal citizen, but rather in terms of their being Adivasis.

This inflection is clearly conveyed in the way Bhimsingh[30] reflected on how he interpreted the knowledge that he acquired about the Indian state and its laws through participating in the AMS:

> We got to know about the rules and the law within our training and we realized that our independence is yet to be completed—it has been left midway only. The country may be independent but we are not ... Our feeling is that our independence is partial till now (interview, March 2010).

Bhimsingh's claim that independence 'is yet to be completed' for Adivasis and that their 'independence is partial till now' suggests that there is something particular about the political subordination of Adivasis that sets them apart from other groups in Indian society, and thus alludes to the particular trajectory of disenfranchisement that has affected Bhil groups in the region.

In the politics of the AMS, this took centre stage in the middle of the 1990s, when the Sangathan moved on from addressing specific forms of exploitation and oppression at the level of the local state to articulating a claim for Adivasi self-rule, reflected in the slogan *hamare gaon mein, hamara raj* (our rule in our villages). In order to pursue this objective, the AMS linked its activities to the Bharat Jan Andolan and its campaign for the implementation of the Bhuriya Committee Report, which had been submitted to the Government of India in 1995, and which argued for the implementation of tribal self-rule in Scheduled Areas. In 1996, the central government enacted the Provisions of the Panchayats (Extension to the Scheduled Areas) Act of 1996, which was intended to devolve powers of governance to the level of the Gram Sabha in Scheduled Areas. When asked to explain why the Sangathan moved in this direction, Bhimsingh responded:

> Anybody who asked for chickens and money, we would give. When this reduced a bit, we became lighter. After that, slowly by going to the meetings, we learnt that this was a big illness. Then they said that our rule means that all of which is there in the village, in our village, our voice should be listened to or heard. Whether it is the *sarkar*[31] or some *neta*,[32] everything should belong to us—then only will our rule be established. This was the Sangathan. After that, the land, jungle and water belong to us. *Bhai*, when you are living here, then everything here including the river and well belong to us. Yes, we do have the right to cut trees; you do not. We have the right to irrigate our lands. You all live there, not here

like us. On everything we should have rights (interview, March 2010).

The rights-based claims that were articulated by the Sangathan were thus not just claims to be recognized as citizens with certain inalienable civil and political liberties. Rather, as the politics of the AMS evolved, they were increasingly articulated in terms of a collective Adivasi identity, in which the central 'loci of consciousness formation' (Harvey 1985: 252) are the dispossession of natural resources—*jal, jangal, zameen* (water, forest, land)—and the claim to have the rights to these resources restored through the restitution of Bhil sovereignty within a determinate territory. In the next section, I explore the ways in which the state responded to the AMS as the movement's demand for self-rule started to gain such momentum that it became a threat to regional power structures.

Countering the Subaltern Advance

By 1996, the AMS had extended its reach across Khargone to encompass more than 500 villages spread across three blocks of the district. At this point, the organizational strength of the Sangathan was such that it was capable of making inroads against liquor sales in the Adivasi villages and against the illegal timber-trade. In so doing, the AMS delivered a direct blow to the incomes of the liquor and timber mafias, as well as to local police and Adivasi *dalals* (power brokers). Importantly, the interests of Jhagdia Patel, president of the Bhagwanpura Congress Committee and hereditary headman of Kabri village, who had profited from illegal trading for a long time, were threatened by these developments.

Further, the enactment of Panchayats (Extension to Scheduled Areas) Act (PESA)[33] in 1996 put a potentially effective tool in the hands of a dynamic organization such as the AMS. What PESA did was to provide the AMS with a means of institutionalizing Adivasi empowerment that was sanctified by the legislative powers of the highest authority in the land. And the fact that the movement was able to rally more than 100,000 people in support of a militant demand for tribal self-rule in the district headquarters cannot but have driven home the point that the AMS was well on its way to becoming a force to be reckoned with in regional politics.

Subhash Yadav, Deputy Chief Minister in Digvijay Singh's Congress government, and MLA from the constituency of Kasaravad in Khargone district, was one of those who took notice of the mounting challenge posed to his position by the AMS. Moving quickly, he struck an alliance with the beleaguered Jhagdia Patel, and orchestrated the formation of an outfit named Adivasi Samaj Sudhar Shanti Sena (ASSSS) to counter the rise of the AMS. What followed was an unprecedented campaign of terror and violent repression in the strongholds of the AMS.[34]

Early in 1996, in Kabri village, activists of the AMS announced that during the Indal festival—the most important annual festival for Adivasis in this region—liquor would not be sold in the village. Jhagdia Patel, the headman of the village, who profited handsomely from liquor sales, took strong exception to this. As retaliation, he and his men kidnapped one of the anti-liquor activists and tortured him by breaking one of his arms and one of his legs. When he begged them to give him a drink of water, they responded by pissing in his mouth. This was followed by several armed attacks on AMS activists, while in Kabri village Jhagdia Patel's men burnt down the houses of anti-liquor activists.

In 1997, the conflict between the AMS and the Shanti Sena intensified. In June of that year, Subhash Yadav turned up at a village meeting in his capacity as Deputy Chief Minister and made a speech in which he accused the Sangathan of being a Naxalite organization involved in sabotaging the government's development projects. If he were Home Minister, he proclaimed, the AMS would have been driven out not just of Madhya Pradesh, but of India altogether. A spate of attacks on AMS activists followed, along with several arrests on false charges.

A more concerted campaign of repression was then implemented after Kaliabhai—an activist in the AMS—mediated in a property dispute in Julwania village. A man who had been fined 35,000 rupees for unlawfully seizing his brother's land had turned to Kaliabhai for assistance. Kaliabhai negotiated with the panchayat that had imposed the fine, and managed to reduce the sum of the fine to 13,000 rupees. However, the man was not satisfied with this outcome, and prodded by local police he filed charges of extortion against Kaliabhai and 29 other AMS activists—none of whom had been involved with the dispute in the first place.

For Jhagdia Patel, this was a golden opportunity to attack the AMS. On August 25, he led a group of men accompanied by a police escort to Kaliabhai's house in Julwania village. Kaliabhai was not at home, but the mob stripped his wife and raped her. Five more women from the village were subjected to the same treatment, but in the aftermath of the attack the police refused to register a case against the perpetrators. The next day, Kaliabhai set out in search of Jhagdia Patel with a group of 150 men. They caught up with him, his posse, and their police escort and surrounded them. The Shanti Sena group took refuge in a nearby house, but as Kaliabhai and his men gathered outside and demanded that Jhagdia Patel be handed over, the police officers opened the door and pushed him out. He was killed with an arrow, and the angry men stoned his dead body.

The police registered cases against more than 80 people for the murder of Jhagdia Patel, and a substantial reward was offered for information about Kaliabhai's whereabouts. Subhash Yadav arrived in Kabri and announced that the state government would give 100,000 rupees to Jhagdia Patel's family as compensation for his death. The next day, Yadav gave a public speech in which he urged the Shanti Sena to recruit more members, and instructed the police to provide five people in each village with guns so as to enable them to counter the AMS. The police subsequently established a camp in Kabri, and the Shanti Sena toured the area. Approximately 400 forest guards accompanied by troops from the Special Action Force and led by the Divisional Forest Officer entered a village in Khandwa district where the residents had refused to pay bribes in order for the forest guards to allow *nevad* cultivation to proceed. They started to uproot the standing crops, and when villagers hurled stones at them to get them to stop, the forest guards and Special Action Force troops opened fire. Two villagers were shot dead and six were injured in the shooting. Nine farmers had their crops razed to the ground in the episode.

A string of arrests in September 1997 prompted leading activists of the AMS to convince Kaliabhai and sixteen other activists to give themselves up to the Deputy Inspector

General of Police in Indore. Two days later, in what proved to be a fateful move, an armed police escort took Kaliabhai with them on an expedition—allegedly to retrieve firearms that were supposed to have been used to murder Jhagdia Patel. As they were on their way back to the police station, the team passed through Kabri—Jhagdia Patel's village—where they were surrounded by a group of 200 people who wanted the police to hand over Kaliabhai to them. Handcuffed and defenseless, Kaliabhai was released to the angry crowd, and was killed with an axe. Amita Baviskar (2001: 16), who took part in a fact-finding mission that investigated the repression of the AMS, has noted there was no good reason for taking Kaliabhai on this expedition: first of all, Jhagdia Patel had been murdered with a bow and arrow, not a firearm, and secondly there was no need to return to the police station via Kabri village. As the report issued by the PUCL in the wake of the killing dryly stated, it was evident that 'there [was] complicity of the police in the custodial death of Kalia' (cited in Baviskar 2001: 16). The repression of the AMS did not end with Kaliabhai's death. Attacks continued into 1998 and the AMS suffered substantial setbacks. Ajaybhai summed up the impact of the repression on the Sangathan as follows: 'In the heydays, we were having more than 60 full-timers; and after that repression, after two years of that repression we slid down to six' (interview, November 2009).

What the repression of the AMS testifies to is the superior capacity of dominant groups to mobilize the power resources that inhere in the institutional ensemble of the state in the face of concerted challenges from below. In the case of the repression of the AMS, political and bureaucratic elites were able to close ranks across spatial scales, from the upper echelons of the state government down to local administration and police, and linked their efforts to the Shanti Sena as an extra-state actor. The capacity of regional elites to orchestrate repression in this manner can only be adequately understood in terms of the way in which state power has been historically constituted in western Madhya Pradesh so as to preserve the hegemony of traditional ruling groups in the postcolonial era in what John Harriss (1999) has called an 'upper caste/class-dominated Congress regime'. As I noted above, the early era of independence witnessed the incorporation of the princely rulers of western Madhya Pradesh into the hegemonic project of the Congress, which in turn enabled them to remain socially and politically dominant in the region. The hegemony of upper castes and classes has persisted since then through their dominance among Congress representatives to the Madhya Pradesh Legislative Assembly, their persistent control of the party machinery, and their predominance among the ministers in the governments formed by Congress between 1956 and 2004 (Jaffrelot 2008).

Whereas Adivasis have been among the most important non-caste groups in Congress politics in Madhya Pradesh, they 'did not form powerful lobbies' (Jaffrelot 2008: 3) capable of disrupting the entrenched balance of power within the party. Indeed, Digvijay Singh's efforts to promote Adivasi leadership within the Congress when he was Chief Minister in the decade from 1993 to 2003 failed even according to his own admission (Jaffrelot 2008). In sum, what this means is that the AMS was mobilizing in relation to a state in which the social power of regional elites was remarkably entrenched, and this in turn came to constitute a barrier that the movement was incapable of moving beyond. I address the strategic ramifications of this in the concluding remarks below.

Concluding Remarks

In chapter I have tried to make a contribution to on going scholarly and activist debates about the strategic role of the state in subaltern politics in India through a substantive analysis of democratic struggles in the Bhil heartland. My point of departure was the adverse incorporation of Bhil communities in the political economy of western India—specifically manifested in the severe and chronic poverty that plagues the Bhil communities of western Madhya Pradesh. I argued that the impact of material deprivation is compounded by political disenfranchisement in the form of a state-society relation that I referred to as 'everyday tyranny'—a predacious and violent regime that denied even the most basic rights and entitlements to Bhil communities in the region.

In the next part of the chapter, I engaged critically with existing perspectives on state-society relations and the dynamics of subaltern politics. Whereas recent Foucauldian studies of relations between the state and subaltern groups in contemporary India have made an important contribution in terms of advancing debates and analyses beyond the increasingly sclerotic frameworks of the Subaltern Studies project, I argued that they still fall short in terms of explaining the complex dialectical interrelationships between conjunctural opportunities and structural constraints in terms of the ways in and extent to which subaltern groups can pursue their oppositional projects in and through the institutions, discourses and technologies of rule of the state. As a suggestion for a possible way of addressing this shortcoming, I outlined the basic elements of a historical-sociological approach that focuses on the mutually constitutive relationship between the micro-politics of state-society relations and the political economy of capitalist development and state formation as master change processes, which I then put to work in an analysis of the historical lineage of everyday tyranny and the contemporary trajectory of Adivasi mobilization in the Bhil heartland.

In terms of the historical origins of everyday tyranny, I argued that these could be traced to the making of colonial state space in the Bhil heartland. Focused on the restructuring of the socioeconomic geography and the consolidation of the modalities of state power, this process not only propelled a process of dispossession that produced the marginal subsistence peasant of today, but also restructured state-society relations in the region in such a way that Bhil communities were politically subordinated to princely rulers with whom they had previously shared sovereignty. As the infrastructural power of the Rajput and Maratha states in the Bhil heartland were developed, the institutional structure through which everyday tyranny would be enacted came into being, turning the state into a feared, unaccountable and rapacious entity. In western Madhya Pradesh this situation was reproduced after independence as the incorporation of princely rulers into the Congress Party allowed them to retain privileged access to the levers of state power.

In the fourth and final part of the chapter, I moved on to a detailed analysis of the mobilizational trajectory of the AMS in the district of Khargone in western Madhya Pradesh. Now, this trajectory provides us with a number of insights that may be of value to a critical discussion of the relationship between subaltern movements and the state in India. The fact that the Sangathan was able to curb the violent excesses and corrupt exactions of local state personnel through a series of militant actions that effected a transformation in emotional dispositions, consciousness and skills, is significant. In many ways the AMS created a new kind of political subject in the communities it mobilized: an assertive and knowledgeable citizen capable of articulating and levelling rights-based claims and holding the state accountable to these. Furthermore, through this democratization of local state-society relations, the AMS also created a 'vernacular rights culture' in which rights-based claims were inflected with a discourse that has been central to modern Adivasi politics across India, in which the historical injustice of dispossession is to be countered through a demand for the recognition of the right to tribal self-rule. Given the point from which the movement started—that is, everyday tyranny—these changes clearly give credence to Corbridge and Harriss's (2000: 239) argument that the state can indeed be 'made to do the bidding of India's lower orders'.

In doing so, the example of the AMS should cause us to be sceptical of those who claim that mobilization centred around 'a pedagogy directed at demystifying the state' (Kamat 2002: 122) will ultimately be unproductive, as it fosters an illusory idea that the state can be harnessed for subaltern projects, and that it is an entity 'which exists for the interests of all people, including that of the poor' (ibid.: 126). Such a perspective smacks of a dogmatic clamour for 'anti-institutional purity' (Poulantzas 1978: 153) that fails to appreciate how significant a subversion of everyday tyranny through the claiming of democratic rights is in its specific context, and how it may be a necessary condition for enabling further mobilization around more radical demands as a movement process unfolds (see Nilsen 2012a: 277-8).

However, the campaign of repression that the AMS was subjected to as it developed into a social and political force that was capable of destabilizing entrenched power relations in the region also suggests that we need to take seriously the limits to the kind of mobilizing strategy that the AMS developed. What this experience of repression demonstrates is of course the superior ability of dominant groups to access certain forms of state power, and to put it to efficient use in bringing an end to the advance of radical subaltern opposition. I have argued elsewhere that an adequate response to this quandary may have to involve a differentiated strategic approach to the state (Nilsen 2012a/b).

On the one hand, it seems clear that much can be gained through the advance of rights-based claims-making in contexts where political subordination takes the form of disenfranchisement and the consistent denial of basic democratic rights, due to the transformations that this kind of mobilization can effect in terms of emotional dispositions and political literacy. Moreover, the everyday victories won through such a strategic repertoire are likely to add momentum to the process of subaltern mobilization. On the other hand, it is also necessary to think about how to circumvent the structural constraints that are intrinsic to a particular form of state. Now, given that state power should be conceived of in terms of 'the power of the social forces which act in and through [the state]' (Jessop 1990: 256), I think it would be quite reasonable to argue that a strategy for achieving this should be geared towards eroding the social basis of elite control over 'the political power that is pre-eminently ascribed to the state' (Poulantzas 1978: 147). Crucially, this entails working towards a political strategy that moves in and against the state at the same time in order to take advantage of the forms of progressive change that can be achieved within its parameters while at the same time developing a counterhegemonic project that has the capacity to challenge existing power relations and their entrenched institutional manifestations.

If we return, finally, to the determinate context in which this chapter is grounded, namely the democratic struggles of local Adivasi movements in western Madhya Pradesh, there is much to suggest that such a strategy would have to entail the building of a dense latticework of subaltern alliances. As I have tried to demonstrate in this chapter, the hegemonic constellations that movements like the AMS are confronting have been constituted through trajectories of state formation that have cemented the power of the upper classes and upper castes in the region. Therefore, developing a counterhegemonic project that transcends the identitarian boundaries of the 'tribal slot' and links the politics of Adivasi movements such as the AMS to a 'war of position' (Gramsci 1998) energized by a broader coalition of subaltern groups may be a *sine qua non* for the future advance of oppositional collective action in the region.

Notes

1. The Bhils are one of the major Adivasi (see note 45 below) groups of western and central India. Consisting of multiple sub-groups such as Bhilalas, Barelas, and Naiks, the Bhils inhabit the largely hilly regions of northeastern Maharashtra, eastern Gujarat, southern Rajasthan and western Madhya Pradesh. For the sake of simplicity, I shall use the term Bhil to refer to Bhils, Bhilalas and Barelas in this chapter. I shall refer to the region they inhabit as the Bhilheart land (see map on page 138).

2. Based on the Madhya Pradesh Human Development Report for 1998, 2002 and 2007. The figures for India are drawn from the UNDP Human Development Reports for the corresponding years. An HDI score between 0.000 and 0.500 is considered to be a low HDI score. There is no data for Alirajpur district, as this district only came into being in 2008.

3. Badwani district was created in 1998, when Khargone district was bifurcated into Badwani and West Nimar. This also explains the sharp rise in HDI score and ranking in West Nimar between 1998 and 2002, as the poorest areas of what was Khargone became part of Badwani district.

4. From Ray et al. (2009: 64).

5. From the India Human Development Report 2011 (GoI 2011: 116).

6. It is worth noting that these estimates are based on the official poverty line proposed by the Planning Commission in 2004-5, according to which 27 per cent of India's population lives in poverty. This poverty line has been widely criticized for being a gross underestimation, and it is therefore likely that the World Bank estimates of Adivasi poverty are too conservative. Nevertheless, this data provides a clear indication of the disproportionate level of poverty among Adivasis as one of India's 'historically marginalized groups' (Mehta and Shah 2003: 502). See Mehta and Venkatraman (2000), Patnaik (2005, 2007, 2010), and Deaton and Kozel (2005) for critiques of the official poverty line suggested by the Planning Commission.

7. See Nilsen (2008, 2010, 2011, 2012a/b) for my previous engagements with this debate.

8. Some representive examples of this body of work include Heller (1999), Jaffrelot (2003), Desai (2007), Fuller and Harriss (2001), Corbridge, Williams, Srivastava and Véron (2005), Sharma (2009), Gupta (1995, 1998, 2001, 2012), Michelutti (2008), Madhok (2003, 2008, 2013) and Williams, Vira and Chopra (2011).

9. See Nilsen (2012b) for a comprehensive discussion of these perspectives.

10. In particular, Harriss and Fuller (2001), Corbridge et al. (2005), Gupta, (1995, 1998, 2001, 2012), Sharma (2008, 2009), Gupta and Sharma (2006, 2008) and Williams, Vira and Chopra (2011).

11. Not his real name. The term 'the people who wear pants' is a reference to state officials of various kinds. In contrast to the Bhils, who mostly wear short-pants or *lungis*, state officials wear pants, shirts and closed shoes, and this is regarded as a key marker of hierarchical difference.

12. Land record officer at sub-district (*tehsil*) level.

13. Officer in charge of the local police station (*thana*).

14. Clarified butter used for cooking.

15. Chillies.

16. Lentils.

17. Not his real name.

18. Not his real name.

19. Not his real name.

20. I owe this term to Prakash Kashwan.

21. See Nilsen (2012c) for an extended discussion of precolonial state-society relationships in India in general and the Bhil heartland more specifically.

22. See Grove (1996), Rangarajan (1999); Sivaramakrishnan (1996, 1998, 1999, 2009), and Gadgil and Guha (1993) on the history of colonial forest policy.

23. See Prakash (2001), Devalle (1992), and the essays collected in Munda and Mullick (2003) on the history of Adivasi mobilization in Jharkhand.

24. These were the Shramik Sangathana (Mies 1986; Basu 1990), the Bhoomi Sena (de Silva, Mehta, Rahman and Wignaraja 1979), and the Kashtakari Sangathana (Kashtakari Sangathana 1986).

25. See Nilsen (2010: Chapter 3) and Baviskar (1995) for detailed accounts of the KMCS.

26. Khargone was divided in 1998, with the western part of the district being named Badwani and the eastern part Khargone.

27. Not his real name.

28. Not his real name.

29. Not her real name.

30. Not his real name.

31. The state.

32. Leader.

33. Footnote explaining what PESA is.

34. I base this account on a series of interviews with AMS activists carried out in 2009 and 2010. In order to reconstruct the detail and sequence of events in the repression of the AMS, I have also drawn extensively on Amita Baviskar's (2001) rich and dense account, which in turn is based on her intervention as a human rights activist during the events of 1997-1998. In addition, I also draw on AMS (1998) and Amnesty International (2000). This account has also been presented in a slightly different form in two previous articles (Nilsen 2012a/b).

Bibliography

Abrams, P. (1982): *Historical Sociology,* Ithaca: Cornell University Press.

Abrams, P. (1988): "Notes on the Difficulty of Studying the State", *Journal of Historical Sociology,* 1/1: 58–89.

Adivasi Mukti Sangathan (n.d.): India: *Reign of Terror Unleashed Against Tribal People and Activists,* AMS, West Nimad (Madhya Pradesh), viewed March 3, 2011, http://www.hrsolidarity.net/mainfile.php/1998vol08no01/1296/.

Agarwala, R. (2008): "Reshaping the Social Contract: Emerging Relations between the State and Informal Labour in India", *Theory and Society,* 37/4: 375–408.

Agarwala, R. (2013): *Informal Labor, Formal Politics, and Dignified Discontent in India,* Cambridge: Cambridge University Press.

Alam, J., (2002): "Peasants, Politics and Historiography: Critique of New Trend in Relation to Marxism", in Ludden, D. (ed.), *Reading Subaltern Studies: Critical History, Contested Meaning and the Globalization of South Asia,* New Delhi: Permanent Black.

Alavi, H. (1965): "Peasants and Revolution", in Miliband, R. and Saville, J. (eds.): *Socialist Register 1965,* London: Merlin Press.

Alirajpur Administrative Report 1869, publisher unknown.

Amin, S. (1984): "Gandhi as Mahatma: Gorakhpur District, Eastern UP, 1921–2", in Ranajit Guha (ed.): *Subaltern Studies III: Writings on Indian History and Society,* Delhi: Oxford University Press.

Amnesty International (n.d.): *Criminalization of Adivasi Rights Activities,* AI, London, viewed March 8, 2011, www.amnesty.org/en/library/asset/ASA20/014/2000/en/d2a8f4e6–df62–11dd-acaa-7d9091d4638f/asa200142000en.html.

Arnold, D. (1982): "Rebellious Hillmen: The Gudem-Rampa Risings, 1924–1939", in Guha, R. (ed.): *Subaltern Studies I: Writings on Indian History and Society*, Delhi: Oxford University Press.

Arnold, D. (1984): "Gramsci and Peasant Subalternity in India", *Journal of Peasant Studies*, 11/4: 155–77.

Asian Human Rights Commission (2012): *India: Homeland Insecurity: Fear of Civil Society in World's Largest Democracy*, AHRC, Kowloon, viewed September 24, 2012, http://www.humanrights.asia/news/urgent-appeals/AHRC-UAG-002-2012.

Bahl, V. (1995): *The Making of the Indian Working Class: The Case of Tata Iron and Steel Company, 1880–1946*, London: Sage.

Banaji, J. (2010): *Theory as History: Essays on Modes of Production and Exploitation*, Leiden: Brill Academic Publishers.

Banerjee, S. (1984): *India's Simmering Revolution: The Naxalite Uprising*, London: Zed Books.

Banerjee-Guha, S. (2008): "Space Relations of Capital and Significance of New Economic Enclaves: SEZs in India", *Economic and Political Weekly*, 43/47, 51–6.

Banerjee-Guha, S. (2011): "Revisiting Accumulation by Dispossession: Neoliberalizing Mumbai", in Banerjee-Guha, S. (ed.): *Accumulation by Dispossession: Transformative Cities in the New Global Order*, Delhi: Sage Publications.

Bardhan, P. (1998): *The Political Economy of Development in India: Expanded Edition*, Delhi: Oxford University Press.

Barker, C. and Cox, L. (2002): *What Have the Romans Ever Done for Us? Academic and Activist Forms of Movement Theorizing*, viewed April 7, 2016, http://www.iol.ie/~mazzoldi/toolsforchange/afpp/afpp8.html.

Baruah, S. (1999): *India Against Itself: Assam and the Politics of Nationality*, New Delhi: Oxford University Press.

Basu, A. (1987): "Grassroots Movements and the State: Reflections on Radical Change in India", *Theory and Society*, 16: 647–674.

Basu, A. (1990): "Indigenous Feminism, Tribal Radicalism and Grass Roots Mobilization in India", *Dialectical Anthropology*, 15/2–3: 193–209.

Basu, S. (2004): *Does Class Matter? Colonial Capital and Workers' Resistance in Bengal, 1890–1937*, Delhi: Oxford University Press.

Bates, C. (1995a): "Lost Innocents and the Loss of Innocence: Interpreting Adivasi Movements in South Asia", in Barnes, R.H., Gray, A. and Kingsbury, B. (eds.): *Indigenous Peoples of Asia*, Ann Arbor: Association for Asian Studies.

Bates, C. (1995b): "Race, Caste, and Tribe In Central India: The Early Origins of Indian Anthropometry", in Robb, P. (ed.): *The Concept of Race in South Asia*, Delhi: Oxford University.

Baviskar, A. (1995): *In the Belly of the River: Tribal Conflicts Over Water in the Narmada Valley*, Delhi: Oxford University Press.

Baviskar, A. (2001): "Written on the Body, Written on the Land: Violence and Environmental Struggles in Central India", University of California Institute of International Studies Working Paper 02–10, Berkeley.

Baviskar, A. (2008): "Contract Killings: Silicosis Among Adivasi Migrant Workers", *Economic and Political Weekly*, 43/25: 8–10.

Baviskar, A. and Sundar, N. (2008): "Democracy versus Economic Transformation?", *Economic and Political Weekly*, 43/46: 83-89.

Berktay, H. (1991): "Three Empires and the Societies They Governed: Iran, India and the Ottoman Empire", *Journal of Peasant Studies*, 18/3–4: 242–63.

Béteille, A. (1986): "The Concept of Tribe with Special Reference to India", *European Journal of Sociology*, 27/2: 296–318.

Bhagwati, J. and Panagariya, A. (2013): *Why Growth Matters: How Economic Growth in India Reduced Poverty and the Lessons for Other Developing Countries*, New York: Public Affairs Books.

Bornstein, E. and Sharma, A. (2016): "The Righteous and the Rightful: The Technomoral Politics of NGOs, Social Movements, and the State in India", *American Ethnologist*, 43/1: 76–90.

Breman, J. (1996): *Footloose Labour: Working in India's Informal Sector*, Cambridge: Cambridge University Press.

Breman, J. (2003): *The Labouring Poor in India: Patterns of Exploitation, Subordination, and Exclusion*, New Delhi: Oxford University Press.

Breman, J. (2010): *Outcast Labour in Asia: Circulation and Informalization of the Workforce at the Bottom of the Economy*, Delhi: Oxford University Press.

Breman, J. (2016): *On Pauperism in Present and Past*, New Delhi: Oxford University Press.

Buttigieg, J. (1995): "Gramsci on Civil Society", *boundary 2*, 22/3: 1-32

Cernea, M. (1999): "Development's Painful Social Costs", in Parasuraman, S., *The Development Dilemma: Displacement in India*, London: Macmillan.

Chakrabarty, D. (1983): "Conditions for Knowledge of Working Class Conditions: Employers, Government and the Jute Workers of

Calcutta, 1890–1940", in Guha, R. (ed.): *Subaltern Studies II: Writings on Indian History and Society* , Delhi: Oxford University Press.

Chakrabarty, D. (1984): "Trade Unions in a Hierarchical Culture: The Jute Workers of Calcutta, 1920–1950", in Guha, R. (ed.): *Subaltern Studies III: Writings on Indian History and Society,* Delhi: Oxford University Press.

Chakrabarty, D. (1995): "Radical Histories and Questions of Enlightenment Rationalism: Some Recent Critiques of Subaltern Studies", *Economic and Political Weekly* 30: 751–759.

Chakrabarty, D. (2000): *Provincializing Europe: Postcolonial Thought and Historical Difference,* Princeton: Princeton University Press.

Chakrabarty, D. (2002): *Habitations of Modernity: Essays in the Wake of Subaltern Studies,* Chicago: University of Chicago Press.

Chakrabarty, D. (2013): "Subaltern Studies in Retrospect and Reminiscence", *Economic and Political Weekly,* 47/12: 23–27.

Chakravarty, M. (2016): "Just How High is Income Inequality in India?",*LiveMint,* 23 May, available at http://www.livemint.com/Opinion/JKZYjYjixRipa95tw2AOXK/Just-how-high-is-income-inequality-in-India.html

Chandavarkar, R. (1994): *The Origins of Industrial Capitalism in India: Business Strategies and the Working Classes in Bombay, 1900–1940,* Cambridge: Cambridge University Press.

Chandavarkar, R. (2000): "The Making of the Working Class: E.P. Thompson and Indian History", in Chaturvedi, V. (ed.): *Mapping Subaltern Studies and the Postcolonial,* London: Verso.

Chandra, U. (2013a): "Negotiating Leviathan: Statemaking and Resistance in the Margins of Modern India", PhD dissertation, Yale University.

Chandra, U. (2013b): "Beyond Subalternity: Land, Community, and the State in Contemporary Jharkhand", *Contemporary South Asia,* 21/1: 52-61

Chatterjee, P. (1982): "Agrarian Relations and Communalism in Bengal, 1926–1935", in Guha, R. (ed.): *Subaltern Studies I: Writings on Indian History and Society,* Delhi: Oxford University Press.

Chatterjee, P. (1983a): "More on Modes of Power and the Peasantry", in Guha, R. (ed.): *Subaltern Studies II: Writings on Indian History and Society,* Delhi: Oxford University Press.

Chatterjee, P. (1983b): "Peasants, Politics and Historiography: A Response", *Social Scientist,* 11/65: 58–65.

Chatterjee, P. (1986) *Nationalist Thought and the Colonial World: A Derivative Discourse,* New Delhi: Oxford University Press.

Chatterjee, P. (1993): *The Nation and its Fragments,* Delhi: Oxford University Press.

Chatterjee, P. (2004): *Politics of the Governed: Reflections on Popular Politics in Most of the World,* New York: Columbia University Press.

Chatterjee, P. (2008): "Democracy and Economic Transformation in India", *Economic and Political Weekly,* 43/16: 53–62.

Chatterjee, P. (2013): "After Subaltern Studies", *Economic and Political Weekly,* 47/35: 44–49.

Chaturvedi, V. (2000a): "Introduction", in Chaturvedi, V. (ed.): *Mapping Subaltern Studies and the Postcolonial,* London: Verso.

Chaturvedi, V. (ed.) (2000b): *Mapping Subaltern Studies and the Postcolonial,* London: Verso.

Chaudhuri, S. (2016): "India's High Growth Rate Isn't Translating to Job Creation", *The Wire,* April 18, available at http://thewire.in/30081/indias-high-growth-rate-isnt-translating-to-job-creation/

Chibber, V. (2013): *Postcolonial Theory and the Spectre of Capital,* London: Verso.

Chopra, D., Williams, B. and Vira, B. (2011): "Politics of Citizenship: Experiencing State-Society Relations from the Margins", *Contemporary South Asia,* 19/3: 243–247.

Chopra, S. (1982): "Missing Correct Perspective", in *Social Scientist,* 10/8: 55–63.

Cooper, F. (2002): "Conflict and Connection: Rethinking Colonial African History", in Ludden, D. (ed.), *Reading Subaltern Studies: Critical History, Contested Meaning and the Globalization of South Asia,* New Delhi: Permanent Black.

Corbridge, S, and Harris, J. (2000): *Reinventing India: Liberalization, Hindu Nationalism and Popular Democracy,* Cambridge, Polity Press.

Corbridge, S. and Shah, A. (2013): "Introduction: The Underbelly of the Indian Boom", *Economy and Society,* 42/3: 335–347

Corbridge, S., Harriss, J. and Jeffrey, C. (2013): *India Today: Economy, Politics and Society,* Cambridge: Polity Press

Corbridge, S., Williams, G., Srivastava, M., and Véron, R. (2005): *Seeing the State: Governance and Governmentality in India,* Cambridge: Cambridge University Press.

Corrigan, P. and Sayer, D. (1985): *The Great Arch: English State Formation as Cultural Revolution,* Oxford: Basil Blackwell.

Cox, L. (1999): *Building Counter Culture: The Radical Praxis of Social Movement Milieux,* unpublished PhD dissertation, Trinity College Dublin.

Cox, L. and Nilsen, A.G. (2014): *We Make Our Own History: Marxism and Social Movements in the Twilight of Neoliberalism,* London: Pluto Press.

Crehan, K. (2002): *Gramsci, Culture and Anthropology,* London: Pluto Press.

Damodaran, V. (2006) "Colonial Constructions of Tribes in India", *Indian Historical Review,* 33/1: 44–76.

Dasgupta, S. (1985): "Adivasi Politics in Midnapur, c. 1760—1924", in Guha, R. (ed.): *Subaltern Studies IV: Writings on Indian History and Society,* Delhi: Oxford University Press.

De Silva, G.V.S., Mehta, N., Rahman. M.A. and Wignaraja. P. (1979): "Bhoomi Sena: A Struggle for People's Power", *Development Dialogue,* 1979/2: 3–40.

Deaton, A. and Kozel, V. (2005): "Data and Dogma: The Great Indian Poverty Debate", *World Bank Research Observer,* 20/2: 177–199.

Desai, M. (2011): *The Rediscovery of India,* London: Bloomsbury Press.

Desai, R. (2016): "The Slow-Motion Counterrevolution: Developmental Contradictions and the Emergence of Neoliberalism", in Nielsen, K.B. and Nilsen, A.G. (eds.): *Social Movements and the State in India: Deepening Democracy?,* London: Palgrave.

Devalle, S.B.C. (1992): *Discourses of Ethnicity: Culture and Protest in Jharkhand,* Delhi: Sage Publications.

Dhagamwar, V. (1997): "The NGO Movements in the Narmada Valley: Some Reflections", in Drèze, J., Samson, M. and Singh, S. (eds.): *The Dam and the Nation: Displacement and Resettlement in the Narmada Valley,* Delhi: Oxford University Press.

Drèze, J. and Sen, A. (2013): *An Uncertain Glory: India and its Contradictions,* London: Penguin.

Duschinski, H. (2009): "Destiny Effects: Militarization, State Power, and Punitive Containment in Kashmir Valley", *Anthropological Quarterly,* 82/3: 691–718.

Dwivedi, R. (1997): People's Movements in Environmental Politics: A Critical Analysis of the Narmada Bachao Andolan in India, Institute of Social Studies Working Paper Series 242, The Hague.

Dwivedi, R. (2006): *Conflict and Collective Action: The Sardar Sarovar Project in India,* London: Routledge.

Escobar, A. (1995): *Encountering Development: The Making and Unmaking of the Third World,* Princeton: Princeton University Press.

Ferguson, J. and Gupta, A. (2002): "Spatializing States: Towards an Ethnography of Neoliberal Governmentality", *American Ethnologist,* 29/4: 981-1002.

Fisher, W.F. (1995): "Development and Resistance in the Narmada Valley", in Fisher, W. F. (ed.): *Towards Sustainable Development? Struggling Over India's Narmada River,*London: M.E. Sharpe.

Foucault, M. (1990): *The History of Sexuality, Volume 1: An Introduction,* New York: Vintage Books.

Foucault, M. (2007): *Security, Territory, Population: Lectures at College de France, 1977-1978,* London: Palgrave.

Foucault, M. (2008): *The Birth of Biopolitics: Lectures at College de France, 1978-1979,* London: Palgrave.

Frankel, F. (2005): *India's Political Economy, 1947–2004: The Gradual Revolution,* New Delhi, Oxford University Press.

Fuller, C. J. and Harriss, J. (2001): "For an Anthropology of the Modern Indian State", in Fuller, C. J. and Béneï, V. (eds.): *The Everyday State and Society in Modern India,* London: Hurst and Company.

Gadgil, M. and Guha, R. (1993): *This Fissured Land: An Ecological History of India,* Delhi: Oxford University Press.

Gathwai, M. (2012): "Externment Notice to MP Activist", *Indian Express,* May 27.

Ghosh, K. (2006): "Between Global Flows and Local Dams: Indigenousness, Locality, and the Transnational Sphere in Jharkhand, India", *Cultural Anthropology,* 21/4: 501-34.

Goswami, M. (2004): *Producing India: From Colonial Economy to National Space,* New Delhi: Permanent Black.

Graham, D.C. (1856): *Historical Sketch of the Bheel Tribes Inhabiting the Province of Khandesh,* Bombay: Government Central Press.

Gramsci, A. (1998): *Selections from the Prison Notebooks,* London: Lawrence and Wishart.

Gramsci, A. (2001): *Selections from Political Writings, 1910-1920,* London: Lawrence and Wishart.

Green, M. (2002): "Gramsci Cannot Speak: Presentations and Interpretations of Gramsci's Concept of the Subaltern", *Rethinking Marxism,* 14/3: 1–24.

Green, M. (2011): "Subaltern Politics", in Kurian, G.T. et al. (eds.): *The Encyclopedia of Political Science,* Washington, DC: CQ Press.

Gudavarthy, A. (ed.) (2012): *Re-framing Democracy and Agency in India: Interrogating Political Society,* London: Anthem Press.

Guha, R. (1982): "On Some Aspects of the Historiography of Colonial India", in Guha, R. (ed.): *Subaltern Studies I: Writings on Indian History and Society,* Delhi: Oxford University Press.

Guha, R. (1983a): *Elementary Aspects of Peasant Insurgency in Colonial India,* Delhi: Oxford University Press.

Guha, R. (1983b): "The Prose of Counter-Insurgency", in Guha, R. (ed.), *Subaltern Studies II: Writings on Indian History and Society,* Delhi: Oxford University Press 1983.

Guha, R. (1989): "Dominance without Hegemony and its Historiography", in Guha, R. (ed.): *Subaltern Studies VI: Writings on Indian History and Society,* Delhi: Oxford University Press.

Guha, R. (1998): *Dominance Without Hegemony: History and Power in Colonial India,* Cambridge: Harvard University Press.

Guha, R. (1985): "Forestry and Social Protest in British Kumaun, c. 1893–1921", in Guha, R. (ed.): *Subaltern Studies IV: Writings on South Asian History and Society,* New Delhi: Oxford University Press.

Guha, R. (2007): "Adivasis, Naxalites and Indian Democracy", *Economic and Political Weekly,* 42/32: 3305–12.

Guha, S. (1999): *Environment and Ethnicity in India, 1200–1991,* Cambridge: Cambridge University Press.

Gupta, A. (1995) "Blurred Boundaries: The Discourse of Corruption, the Culture of Politics, and the Imagined State", *American Ethnologist,* 22/2: 375–402.

Gupta, A. (1998): *Postcolonial Developments: Agriculture in the Making of Modern India,* Durham: Duke University Press.

Gupta, A. (2001): "Governing Population: The Integrated Child Development Services Program in India", in Hansen, T.B. and Stepputat, F. (eds.): *States of Imagination: Ethnographic Explorations of the Postcolonial State,* Durham: Duke University Press.

Gupta, A. (2012): *Red Tape: Bureaucracy, Structural Violence and Poverty in India,* Durham: Duke University Press.

Gupta, A. and Sharma, A. (2006a): "Globalization and Postcolonial States", *Current Anthropology,* 47/2: 277–307.

Gupta, A. and Sharma, A. (2006b): "Introduction: Rethinking Theories of the State in an Age of Globalization", in Gupta, A. and Sharma, A. (eds.): *Anthropology of the State: A Reader*, Oxford: Wiley-Blackwell.

Gupta, D. (2010): *Caged Phoenix: Can India Fly?*, New Delhi: Penguin Books.

Gupta, D. (2013): *Revolution From Above: India's Future and the Citizen Elite*, New Delhi: Rupa Books.

Guruswamy, M. (2016): "It's All in the Numbers: Don't Celebrate India's GDP Growth Yet", Scroll.in, June 5, available at http://scroll.in/article/809313/its-all-in-the-numbers-dont-celebrate-indias-gdp-growth-yet.

Haldon, J.F. (1993): *The State and the Tributary Mode of Production*, London: Verso.

Hardiman, D. (1984): "Adivasi Assertion in South Gujarat: The Devi Movement of 1922—3", in Ranajit Guha (ed.): *Subaltern Studies III: Writings on Indian History and Society*, Delhi: Oxford University Press.

Hardiman, D. (1987a): *The Coming of the Devi: Adivasi Assertion in Western India*, Delhi: Oxford University Press.

Hardiman, D. (1987b), "The Bhils and Shahukars of Eastern Gujarat", in Guha, R. (ed.): *Subaltern Studies V: Writings on Indian History and Society*, Delhi: Oxford University Press.

Harriss, J. (1999): "Comparing Political Regimes Across Indian States: A Preliminary Essay", *Economic and Political Weekly*, 34/48: 3367–77.

Harriss, J. (2011a): "How Far Have India's Economic Reforms Been "Guided by Compassion and Justice"?, in Ruparelia, S., Reddy, S., Harriss, J. and Corbridge, S. (eds.): *Understanding India's New Political Economy: A Great Transformation?*, London: Routledge.

Harriss, J. (2011b): "What is Going On in India's 'Red Corridor'? Questions About India's Maoist insurgency", *Pacific Affairs*, 84/2: 309–27.

Harriss, J. (2015) "Hindu Nationalism in Action: The Bharatiya Janata Party and Indian Politics", *South Asia*, 38/4: 712–718.

Harriss-White, B. (2003): *India Working: Essays on Society and Economy*, Cambridge: Cambridge University Press.

Harvey, D. (1985): *Consciousness and the Urban Experience: Studies in the History and Theory of Capitalist Urbanization*, Oxford: Basil Blackwell.

Harvey, D. (1996): *Justice, Nature and the Geography of Difference*, Oxford: Blackwell.

Harvey, D. (2003): *The New Imperialism*, London: Oxford University Press.

Heller, P. (1999): *The Labor of Development: Workers and the Transformation of Capitalism in Kerala, India,* Ithaca: Cornell University Press.

Hickey, S. (2010): "The Government of Chronic Poverty: From Exclusion to Citizenship?",*Journal of Development Studies,* 46/7: 1139–1155.

Hickey, S. and Bracking, S. (2005): "Exploring the Politics of Chronic Poverty: From Representation to a Politics of Justice?",*World Development,* 33/6: 851–65.

Hickey, S. and du Toit, A. (2007): "Adverse Incorporation, Social Exclusion and Chronic Poverty", Chronic Poverty Research Centre Working Paper 81, Manchester.

Hill, C. (1991): *The World Turned Upside Down: Radical Ideas During the English Revolution,* London: Penguin Books.

Hobsbawm, E.J. (1965): *Primitive Rebels: Studies in Archaic Forms of Social Movement in the Nineteenth and Twentieth Centuries.* London: W. W. Norton.

Hobsbawm, E.J. (1973): "Peasants and Politics", *Journal of Peasant Studies,* 1/1: 3–22.

Jaffrelot, C. (2003): *The Silent Revolution: The Rise of the Lower Castes in North India,* London: C. Hurst and Co.

Jaffrelot, C. (2008): "The Uneven Plebeianisation of Madhya Pradesh Politics", *Seminar* 591, available at http://www.india-seminar.com/2008/591.htm.

Jaffrelot, C. (2015): "The Modi-centric BJP 2014 Election Campaign: New Techniques and Old Tactics", *Contemporary South Asia,* 23/2: 151–166.

Jayadev, A., Motiram, S., and Vakulabharanam (2011): "Patterns of Wealth Disparities in India Since the 1990s", in Ruparelia, S., Reddy, S., Harriss, J. and Corbridge, S. (eds.): *Understanding India's New Political Economy: A Great Transformation?,* London: Routledge.

Jayal, N.G. (2000): *Democracy and the State: Welfare, Secularism and Development in Contemporary India,* Delhi: Oxford University Press.

Jeffrey, C. (2001): "'A Fist is Stronger than Five Fingers': Caste and Dominance in Rural North India", *Transactions of the Institute of British Geographers,* 26/2: 217-236.

Jeffrey, C. and Lerche, J. (2001): "Dimensions of Dominance: Class and State in Uttar Pradesh", in Fuller, C.J. and Benei, V. (eds.): *The Everyday State and Society in Modern India,* London: Hurst and Company.

Jessop, B. (1982): *The Capitalist State: Marxist Theories and Methods,* Oxford: Martin Robertson.

Jessop, B. (1990): *State Theory: Putting the Capitalist State in its Place,* Cambridge: Polity Press.

Jessop, B. (2008): *State Power,* Cambridge: Polity Press.

Joseph, G. and Nugent, D. (1994): "Popular Culture and State Formation in Revolutionary Mexico", in Gilbert, J. and Nugent, D. (eds.): *Everyday Forms of State Formation: Revolution and the Negotiation of Rule in Modern Mexico,* Durham: Duke University Press.

Kala, P. (2001): "In the Spaces of Erasure: Globalisation, Resistance and Narmada River", *Economic and Political Weekly,* 36/22: 1991–2002.

Kalyvas, A. (2002): "The Stateless Theory: Poulantzas' Challenge to Postmodernism", in Aronowitz, S. and Bratsis, P. (eds.): *Paradigm Lost: State Theory Reconsidered,* Minneapolis: University of Minnesota Press.

Kamat, S. (2002): *Development Hegemony: NGOs and the State in India,* Delhi: Oxford University Press.

Kashtakari Sangathana (1986): "Kashtakari Sangathana (the Warli Uprising Revisited)", in Desai, A. R. (ed.): *Agrarian Struggles in India After Independence,* Delhi: Oxford University Press.

Katzenstein, M. and Ray, R. (2005): "And in the Beginning There Was the Nehruvian State", in Ray, R. and Katzenstein, M. (eds.): *Social Movements in India: Poverty, Power, and Politics,* Rowman and Littlefield.

Kaviraj, S. (1997): "A Critique of the Passive Revolution", in Chatterjee, P. (ed.): *State and Politics in India,* Delhi: Oxford University Press.

Kaviraj, S. (2010): *The Imaginary Institution of India: Politics and Ideas,* New York: Columbia University Press.

Kaviraj, S. (2012a): *The Trajectories of the Indian State: Politics and Ideas,* Delhi: Permanent Black.

Kaviraj, S. (2012b): *The Enchantment of Democracy and India: Politics and Ideas,* Delhi: Permanent Black.

Kela, S. (2012): *A Rogue and Peasant Slave: Adivasi Resistance, 1800–2000,* New Delhi: Navayana.

Khagram, S. (2004): *Dams and Development: Transnational Struggles for Water and Power,* Ithaca: Cornell University Press.

Klingensmith, D. (2007): *One Valley and a Thousand: Dams, Nationalism, and Development,* Delhi: Oxford University Press.

Kohli, A. (2006a): "Politics of Economic Growth in India, 1980–2005: Part 1: The 1980s", *Economic and Political Weekly,* April 1: 1251–59.

Kohli, A. (2006b): "Politics of Economic Growth in India, 1980–2005: Part 2: The 1990s and Beyond", *Economic and Political Weekly,* April 8: 1363–71.

Kohli, A. (2012): *Poverty Amid Plenty in the New India,* Cambridge: Cambridge University Press.

Krishnan, U. and Antony, A. (2016): "Modi Rebuts Analysts Who Doubt India's World-Beating Growth", Bloomberg, March 28, available at http://www.bloomberg.com/news/articles/2016–03–28/modi-rebuts-economists-who-doubt-india-s-world-beating-growth

Levien, M. (2012): "The Land Question: Special Economic Zones and the Political Economy of Dispossession in India", *Journal of Peasant Studies,* 39/3–4: 933–969.

Levien, Michael (2013): The Politics of Dispossession: Theorizing India's "Land Wars", *Politics & Society,* Vol. 41 No. 3: 351–394.

Li, T. M. (1999): "Articulating Indigenous Identity in Indonesia: Resource Politics and the Tribal Slot", *Comparative Studies in Society and History,* 42/1: 149–79.

Ludden, D. (2003): "Introduction: A Brief History of Subalternity", in Ludden, D. (ed.): *Reading Subaltern Studies: Critical History, Contested Meaning and the Globalization of South Asia,* New Delhi: Permanent Black.

Madhok, S. (2003): "A 'Limited Women's Empowerment': Politics, the State, and Development in North West India", *Women's Studies Quarterly,* 31/3–4: 154–173.

Madhok, S. (2010): "Poverty, Entitlement and Citizenship: Vernacular Rights Cultures in Southern Asia", in Chant, S. (ed.): *The International Handbook on Gender and Poverty,* London: Edward Elgar, London.

Madhok, S. (2013): *Rethinking Agency: Developmentalism, Gender and Rights,* New Delhi: Routledge.

Mallet, V. (2016): "Faster Growing India Confirmed as Most Dynamic Emerging Market", *Financial Times,* May 31, available at http://www.ft.com/cms/s/0/06b63142–2748–11e6–8ba3–cdd781d02d89.html#axzz4JBwJUlzL

Mallon, F.E. (1994): "Reflections on the Ruins: Everyday Forms of State Formation in Nineteenth Century Mexico", in Gilbert, J. and Nugent, D. (eds.): *Everyday Forms of State Formation: Revolution and the Negotiation of Rule in Modern Mexico,* Durham: Duke University Press.

Mallon, F.E. (1995): *Peasant and Nation: The Making of Postcolonial Mexico and Peru*, Berkeley: University of California Press.

Mann, M. (1984): "The Autonomous Power of the State: Its Origins, Mechanisms and Results", *European Journal of Sociology*, 25/2: 185–213.

Manning, B. (1996): *Aristocrats, Plebeians and Revolution in England 1640–1660*, London: Pluto Press.

Manning, B. (1999): *The Far Left in the English Revolution*, London: Bookmarks.

Marx, K. (1984): *The Eighteenth Brumaire of Louis Napoleon*, London: Lawrence and Wishart.

Mathur, L.P. (1988): *Resistance Movement of Tribals of India: A Case Study of the Bhils of Rajasthan in the Nineteenth Century*, Udaipur: Himanshu Publications.

Mehta, A.K., Shepherd, A., Bhide, S., Shah, A. and Kumar, A. (2011): *India Chronic Poverty Report: Towards Solutions and New Compacts in a Dynamic Context*, New Delhi: Indian Institute of Public Administration.

Mehta, J. and Venkatraman, S. (2000): "Poverty Statistics: Bermicide's feast", *Economic and Political Weekly*, 35 (27): 2377–2382.

Michelutti, L. (2008): *The Vernacularization of Democracy: Politics, Caste and Religion in India*, Delhi: Routledge.

Mies, M. (1986): "The Shahada Movement: A Peasant Movement in Maharashtra (India)—Its Development and Its Perspectives", in Desai, A.R. (ed.): *Agrarian Struggles in India After Independence*, Delhi: Oxford University Press.

Moore, D.S. (1998): "Subaltern Struggles and the Politics of Place: Remapping Resistance in Zimbabwe's Eastern Highlands", *Cultural Anthropology*, 13/3: 344-81.

Moore, D.S. (2000): "The Crucible of Cultural Politics: Reworking 'Development' in Zimbabwe's Eastern Highlands", *American Ethnologist*, 26/3: 654–89.

Moore, D.S. (2003): "Beyond Blackmail: Multivalent Modernities and the Cultural Politics of Development in India", in K. Sivaramakrishnan, and A. Agrawal (eds.): *Regional Modernities: The Cultural Politics of Development in India*. Stanford: Stanford University Press.

Morton, A.D. (2007): *Unravelling Gramsci: Hegemony and Passive Revolution in the Global Economy*, London: Pluto Press.

Mosse, D. (2007): "Power and the Durability of Poverty: A Critical Exploration of the Links Between Culture, Marginality and Chronic Poverty", Manchester: Chronic Poverty Research Centre.

Mosse, D. (2010): "A Relational Approach to Durable Poverty, Inequality and Power", *Journal of Development Studies*, 46 (7): 1156–1178.

Mosse, D., Gupta, S. and Shah, V. (2005): "On the Margins in the City: Adivasi Seasonal Labour Migration in Western India", *Economic and Political Weekly*, 40/28: 3025–38.

Mosse, D., Gupta, S., Mehta, M., Shah, V. and Rees, J. (2002): "Brokered Livelihoods: Debt, Labour Migration and Development in Tribal Western India", *Journal of Development Studies*, 38/5: 59–88.

Mukherji, N. (2012): *The Maoists in India: Tribals Under Siege*, London: Pluto Press.

Munda, R.D. and Mullick, S.B. (eds.) (2003): *The Jharkhand Movement: Indigenous People's Struggle for Autonomy in India*, Copenhagen: IWGIA.

Nayyar, D. (2006): "India's Unfinished Journey: Transforming Growth into Development", *Modern Asian Studies*, 40/3: 797–832.

NBA (1988): "The Statement Issued by Organization in Narmada Valley to Oppose Sardar Sarovar Project, on August 18, 1988", in Sangvai, S. (2000): *The River and Life: People's Struggle in the Narmada Valley*, Mumbai: Earthcare Books.

NBA (1992): *Towards Just and Sustainable Development: The People's Struggle in the Narmada Valley*, Baroda (Gujarat): NBA.

NBA (2000a): *People vs. Verdict*, Vadodara: NBA.

NBA (2000b): "September 17, Conclusion of Narmada Satyagraha, Jalsindhi and Domkhedi", press release, September 16, 2000.

Ness, I. (2015): *Southern Insurgency: The Coming of the Global Working Class*, London: Pluto Press.

Nilsen, A.G. (2007): "On New Social Movements and 'the Reinvention of India'", *Forum for Development Studies*, 2: 271–293.

Nilsen, A.G. (2008): "Political Economy, Social Movements and State Power: A Marxian Perspective on Two Decades of Resistance to the Narmada Projects", *Journal of Historical Sociology*, 21/2–3: 303–330.

Nilsen, A.G. (2009): "'The Authors and the Actors of Their Own Drama': Towards a Marxist Theory of Social Movements", *Capital and Class*, 33/3: 109–139.

Nilsen, A.G. (2010): *Dispossession and Resistance in India: The River and the Rage*, London: Routledge.

Nilsen, A.G. (2011): "'Not Suspended in Mid-Air': Critical Reflections on Subaltern Encounters with the Indian State", in Motta, S.M. and Nilsen, A.G. (eds.): *Social Movements in the Global South: Dispossession, Development and Resistance,* Basingstoke: Palgrave Macmillan.

Nilsen, A.G. (2012a): "Adivasis In and Against the State: Subaltern Politics and State Power in Contemporary India", *Critical Asian Studies,* 44/2: 251–82.

Nilsen, A.G. (2012b): 'Subalternity and Resistance in the Adivasi Heartland', paper presented to the Politics and Protest Workshop, CUNY Graduate Center, viewed on April 7, 2016, http://politicsandprotest.ws.gc.cuny.edu/archives/fall-2012/.

Nilsen, A.G. (2014): "Postcolonial Social Movements", in Ness, I. and Cope, Z. (eds.): *The Palgrave Encyclopedia of Imperialism and Anti-Imperialism,* New York: Palgrave Macmillan.

Nilsen, A.G. (2015): "For a Historical Sociology of State-Society Relations in the Study of Subaltern Politics", in Nilsen, A. G. and Roy, S. (eds.): *New Subaltern Politics: Reconceptualizing Hegemony and Resistance in Contemporary India,* New Delhi: Oxford University Press.

Nilsen, A.G. and Cox, L. (2013): 'What Would a Marxist Theory of Social Movements Look Like?', in Barker, C., Cox, L., Krinsky, J. and Nilsen, A.G. (eds.): *Marxism and Social Movements,* Leiden: Brill.

Nilsen, A.G. and Roy, S. (2015): "Reconceptualizing Subaltern Politics in Contemporary India", in Nilsen, A. G. and Roy, S. (eds.): *New Subaltern Politics: Reconceptualizing Hegemony and Resistance in Contemporary India,* New Delhi: Oxford University Press.

Nugent, D. and Alonso, A.M. (1994): "Multiple Selective Traditions in Agrarian Reform and Agrarian Struggle: Popular Culture and State Formation in the *Ejido* of Namiquipa", in Gilbert, J. and Nugent, D. (eds.): *Everyday Forms of State Formation: Revolution and the Negotiation of Rule in Modern Mexico,* Durham: Duke University Press.

O'Hanlon, R. (2002): "Recovering the Subject: Subaltern Studies and Histories of Resistance in Colonial South Asia",in Ludden, D. (ed.), *Reading Subaltern Studies: Critical History, Contested Meaning and the Globalization of South Asia,* New Delhi: Permanent Black.

O'Hanlon, R. and Washbrook, D. (1992): "After Orientalism: Culture, Criticism, and Politics in the Third World", *Comparative Studies in Society and History,* 34/1: 134–67.

Omvedt, G. (1993): *Reinventing Revolution: New Social Movements and the Socialist Tradition in India,* New York, East Gate.

OPHDI (2015): OPHI Country Briefing December 2015: India, retrieved from http://www.ophi.org.uk/multidimensional-poverty-index/mpi-2015/mpi-country-briefings/

Outram, J. (1853): *A Memoir of the Public Services Rendered by Lieut. Colonel Outram, C.B.,*London: Smith, Elder and Company.

Padel, F. and Das, S. (2010): *Out of This Earth: East India Adivasis and the Aluminium Cartel,* New Delhi: Orient BlackSwan.

Palit, C. (2003): "Monsoon Risings: Mega-Dam Resistance in the Narmada Valley", *New Left Review,* 21: 81–100.

Palshikar, S. (2016): "Who is Delhi's Common Man?", *New Left Review* 98, 113–128.

Pandey, G. (1978): *The Ascendancy of the Congress in Uttar Pradesh 1926–34: A Study in Imperfect Mobilization,* Delhi: Oxford University Press.

Pandey, G. (1982): "Peasant Revolt and Indian Nationalism: The Peasant Movement in Awadh, 1919–22", in Guha, R. (ed.): *Subaltern Studies I: Writings on Indian History and Society,* Delhi: Oxford University Press.

Parajuli, P. (1992): "Power and Knowledge in Development Discourse: New Social Movements and the State in India", *International Social Science Journal,* 127: 173–190.

Parasuraman, S. (1997): "The Anti-Dam Movement and Rehabilitation Policy", in Drèze, J., Samson, M., and Singh, S. (eds.): *The Dam and the Nation: Displacement and Resettlement in the Narmada Valley,*Delhi: Oxford University Press.

Parasuraman, S. (1999): *The Development Dilemma: Displacement in India,* London: Macmillan Press.

Parry, J. (2014): "Introduction: On the Persistence of Poverty in India", in Gooptu, N. and Parry, J. (eds.): *Persistence of Poverty in India,* New Delhi: Social Science Press.

Patel, A. (1995): "What Do the Narmada Valley Tribals Want?", in Fisher, W. F. (ed.): *Towards Sustainable Development? Struggling Over India's Narmada River,* London: M.E. Sharpe.

Patel, A. (1997): "Resettlement Politics and Tribal Interest", in Drèze, J., Samson, M., and Singh, S. (eds.): *The Dam and the Nation: Displacement and Resettlement in the Narmada Valley,* Delhi: Oxford University Press.

Patkar, M. (1995): "The Struggle for Participation and Justice: A Historical Narrative", in Fisher, W.F. (ed.): *Towards Sustainable Development? Struggling Over India's Narmada River,* London: M.E. Sharpe.

Patnaik, U. (2005): "Theorizing Food Security and Poverty in the Era of Neoliberal Reforms", *Social Scientist,* 33/7–8: 50–81.

Patnaik, U. (2007): "Neoliberalism and Rural Poverty in India", *Economic and Political Weekly,* 42/30: 3132–3150.

Patnaik, U. (2010) "Trends in Urban Poverty under Economic Reforms: 1993–94 to 2004–05", *Economic and Political Weekly,* 45/4: 42–53.

Poulantzas, N. (1978): *State, Power, Socialism,* London: Verso Books.

Prakash, A. (2001): *Jharkhand: Politics of Development and Ethnicity,* Hyderabad: Orient Longman.

Prakash, G. (1990): "Writing Post-Orientalist Histories of the Third World: Perspectives from Indian Historiography", *Comparative Studies in Society and History,* 32/2: 383–408.

Prakash, G. (1992a): "Postcolonial Criticism and Indian Historiography", *Social Text,* 31–32: 8–19.

Prakash, G. (1992b): "Can the 'Subaltern' Ride? A Reply to O'Hanlon and Washbrook", *Comparative Studies in Society and History,* 34/1: 168–184.

Prakash, G. (1994): "Subaltern Studies as Postcolonial Criticism", *American Historical Review,* 99: 1475–1490.

Prasad, A. (2004): *Environmentalism and the Left: Contemporary Debates and Future Agendas in Tribal Areas,* New Delhi, Leftword.

Rangachari, R., Sengupta, N., Iyer, R.R., Banerji, P. and Singh, S. (2000): *Large Dams: India's Experience,* Case Study Prepared for the World Commission on Dams, Cape Town.

Rangan, H. (1996): "From Chipko to Uttaranchal: Development, Environment and Social Protest in the Garhwal Himalayas, India", in Peet, R. and Watts, M. (ed.): *Liberation Ecologies: Environment, Development and Social Movements,* London: Routledge .

Rangan, H. (2000): *Of Myths and Movements: Rewriting Chipko into Himalayan History,* New Delhi: Oxford University Press.

Roseberry, W. (1994): "Hegemony and the Languages of Contention", in Joseph, G.M. and Nugent, D. (eds.): *Everyday Forms of State Formation: Revolution and the Negotiation of Rule in Everyday Mexico,* Durham: Duke University Press.

Roy, A. (2002): *The Algebra of Infinite Justice,* New Delhi: Penguin.

Roy, S. (2014): "New Activist Subjects: The Changing Feminist Field of Kolkata, India", *Feminist Studies,* 40/3: 628–656.

Roy, S. (2015): "The Indian Women's Movement: Within and Beyond NGOization", *Journal of South Asian Development,* 10/1: 96–117.

Ruparelia, S. (2013): India's New Rights Agenda: Genesis, Promises, Risks, *Pacific Affairs* 86/3: 569–590.

Ruparelia, S. (2015): "'Minimum Government, Maximum Governance': The Restructuring of Power in Modi's India", in *South Asia*, 38/4: 755–775.

Sah, D.C., Bhatt, A. and Dalapati, T.K. (n.d.): Chronic Poverty in Tribal Areas of Gujrat, Rajasthan, Madhya Pradesh, Jharkhand and Chhattisgarh, unpublished research report.

Sangvai, S. (2000): *The River and Life: People's Struggle in the Narmada Valley*, Kolkata: Earthcare Books.

Sarkar, S. (1983): *Modern India, 1885–1947*, London: Macmillan.

Sarkar, S. (1984): "The Conditions and Nature of Subaltern Militancy: Bengal from Swadeshi to Non-Cooperation, c. 1905–22", in Ranajit Guha (ed.): *Subaltern Studies III: Writings on Indian History and Society*, Delhi: Oxford University Press.

Sarkar, S. (1994): "Orientalism Revisited: Saidian Frameworks in the Writing of Modern Indian History", *Oxford Literary Review*, 16: 205–224.

Sarkar, S. (2000): *Writing Social History*, Delhi, Oxford University Press.

Sarkar, S. (2002): "The Decline of the Subaltern in Subaltern Studies", in Ludden, D. (ed.): *Reading Subaltern Studies: Critical History, Contested Meaning and the Globalization of South Asia*, New Delhi: Permanent Black.

Sarkar, T. (1985): "Jitu Santal's Movement in Malda, 1924–32: A Study in Tribal Protest", in Guha, R. (ed.): *Subaltern Studies IV: Writings on Indian History and Society*, Delhi: Oxford University Press.

Scott, J.C. (1976): *The Moral Economy of the Peasant: Rebellion and Subsistence in Southeast Asia*, New Haven: Yale University Press.

Scott, J.C. (1990): *Domination and the Arts of Resistance: Hidden Transcripts*, New Haven: Yale University Press.

Scott, J.C. (2010): *The Art of Not Being Governed: An Anarchist History of Upland Southeast Asia*, New Haven: Yale University Press.

Sen, A. and Drèze, J. (2013): *An Uncertain Glory: India and its Contradictions*, New Delhi: Penguin Books.

Sen, H. (2005a): "The Bhils in Colonial Mewar", mimeo.

Sen, H. (2005b): "The Bhil Rebellion of 1881", mimeo.

Sewell, W. (1992): "A Theory of Structure: Duality, Agency, and Transformation", *American Journal of Sociology*, 98/1: 1-29

Shah, A. (2007a) "The Dark Side of Indigeneity: Indigenous People, Rights and Development in India", *History Compass*, 5/6: 1806–32.

Shah, A. (2007b): "Keeping the State Away': Democracy, Politics, and the State in India's Jharkhand", *Journal of the Royal Anthropological Institute,* 13/1: 129–45.

Shah, A. (2010): *In the Shadows of the State: Indigenous Politics, Enviromentalism, and Insurgency in Jharkhand, India,* Durham: Duke University Press.

Sharma, A. (2008): *The Logics of Empowerment: Development, Gender and Governance in Neoliberal India,* Minneapolis: University of Minnesota Press.

Simcox, A.H.A. (1912): *A Memoir of the Khandesh Bhil Corps: 1825–1891,* Bombay: Thacker and Company.

Singh, C.S.K. (1995): *The Sound of Drums: Tribal Movement in Rajasthan, 1881–1947,* New Delhi: Manak Publications.

Singh, K S. (1978): "Colonial Transformation of Tribal Society in Middle India", *Economic and Political Weekly,* 13/30: 1221–1232.

Singh, K.S. (1985): *Tribal Society in India: An Anthropo-Historical Perspective,* Delhi: Manohar.

Singh, M.P. (2009a): "Malnutrition Reaches Epidemic Proportions in Madhya Pradesh.", *The Hindu,* November 27.

Singh, M.P. (2009b): "Madhya Pradesh Clueless as Children Die of Malnutrition", *The Hindu,* August 1, 2009.

Singh, M.P. (2010a): "Report Paints Bleak Picture of Hunger and Malnutrition in Madhya Pradesh", *The Hindu,* 19 February.

Singh, M.P. (2010b): "Madhya Pradesh Child Mortality Rate is One of the Highest in the World, Says Report", *The Hindu,* February 22.

Singh, M.P. (2011a): "Death as Destiny for Migrant Labourers of Alirajpur", *The Hindu,* April 16.

Singh, M.P. (2011b): "Spewing Silicosis: Gujarat's Factories of Doom", *The Hindu,* May 5.

Singh, S. (1997): *Taming the Waters: The Political Economy of Large Dams in India,* Delhi: Oxford University Press.

Sinha, S. (2004): "Development Counter-Narratives: Taking Social Movements Seriously", in Sivaramakrishnan, K. and Agrawal, A. (eds.), *Regional Modernities: The Cultural Politics of Development in India,* Stanford: Stanford University Press.

Sinha, S. (2006): "New Subalterns and Development Discourses: Translation, Intelligibility, Mainstreaming", paper presented to Norsk Forening for Utviklingsforskning Conference, Oslo.

Sinha, S. (2012): "The Long March from the Margins: Subaltern Politics, Justice and Nature in Postcolonial India", in Balibar, E., Mezzadra, S. and Sammadar, R. (eds.): *The Borders of Justice*, Philadelphia: Temple University Press.

Sivaramakrishnan, K. (2002), "Situating the Subaltern: History and Anthropology in the Subaltern Studies Project", in Ludden, D. (ed.): *Reading Subaltern Studies: Critical History, Contested Meaning and the Globalization of South Asia*, New Delhi: Permanent Black.

Skaria, A. (1998): "Being Jangli: The Politics of Wildness", *Studies in History*, 14/2: 193–215.

Skaria, A. (1999): *Hybrid Histories: Forests, Frontiers and Wildness in Western India*, Delhi: Oxford University Press.

Skirbekk, G. (1984): *Ord: Essay i Utval*, Oslo: Samlaget.

Spivak, G.C. (1985): "Subaltern Studies: Deconstructing Historiography", in Guha, R. (ed.): *Subaltern Studies IV: Writings on Indian History and Society*, Delhi: Oxford University Press.

Spivak, G.C. (1988): "Can the Subaltern Speak?", in Nelson, C. and Grossberg, L. (eds.): *Marxism and the Interpretation of Culture*, London: Macmillan.

Steinberg, M. (1994a): "The Dialogue of Struggle: The Contest Over Ideological Boundaries in the Case of London Silk Weavers in the Early Nineteenth Century", *Social Science History*, 18/4: 505–541.

Steinberg, M. (1994b): "The Talk and Back Talk of Collective Action: A Dialogic Analysis of Repertoires of Discourse Among Nineteenth-Century English Cotton Spinners", *American Journal of Sociology*, 105/3: 736–780.

Subramanian, A. (2003): "Modernity From Below: Local Citizenship on the South Indian Coast", *International Social Science Journal*, 55/175: 135–44.

Subramanian, A. (2009): *Shorelines: Space and Rights in South India*, Stanford: Stanford University Press.

Sundar, N. (2007): *Subalterns and Sovereigns: An Anthropological History of Bastar (1854–2005)—Second Edition*, New Delhi: Oxford University Press.

Sundar, N. (2011): "The Rule of Law and Citizenship in India: Post-Colonial Dilemmas", *Citizenship Studies*, 15/3–4: 419–32.

Sundar, N. (2012): "Insurgency, Counter-insurgency, and Democracy in Central India", in Jeffrey, R., Sen, R. and Singh, P. (eds.): *More*

Than Maoism: Politics, Policies, and Insurgencies in South Asia, New Delhi: Manohar Publishers.

Tharu, S. (2016): "The Promise and the Lie of the University", Tehelka, February 9, available at http://www.tehelka.com/2016/02/the-promise-and-the-lie-of-the-university/

Thomas, P.D. (2009): *The Gramscian Moment: Philosophy, Hegemony, and Marxism,* Leiden: Brill Publications.

Thomas, P.D. (2013): "Hegemony, Passive Revolution and the Modern Prince", *Thesis 11,* 117: 20–39.

Thompson, E.P. (1968): *The Making of the English Working Class,* New York: Vintage.

Thompson, E.P. (1971): "The Moral Economy of the English Crowd in the Eighteenth Century", *Past and Present* 50: 76–136.

Thompson, E.P. (1975): *Whigs and Hunters: The Origins of the Black Act,* London: Penguin.

Thompson, E.P. (1978): "Eighteenth Century English Society: Class Struggle Without Class", *Social History,* 3/2: 133 165.

Tilly, C. (1982): *As Sociology Meets History,* New York: Academic Press.

Tilly, C. (1984): *Big Structures, Large Processes, Huge Comparisons,* New York: Russell Sage Foundation.

Tilly, C., Tilly, L. and Tilly, R. (1975): *The Rebellious Century, 1830–1930,* Cambridge, MA: Harvard University Press.

Tripathy, R. (2015): "How Modi-Speak Boomeranged in Bihar", *Economic and Political Weekly,* 50/46–47: 13–16.

UNDP (2013): *Human Development Report 2013—The Rise of the South: Human Progress in a Diverse World,* New York: United Nations Development Programme.

Vanaik, A. (1990): *The Painful Transition: Bourgeois Democracy in India,* London, Verso.

Vanaik, A. (2001): "The New Indian Right", *New Left Review* 9: 43–67.

Waghmore, S. (2013): *Civility Against Caste: Dalit Politics and Citizenship in Western India,* New Delhi: Sage Publications.

Walker, K.L.M. (2008): "Neoliberalism on the Ground in Rural India: Predatory Growth, Agrarian Crisis, Internal Colonization, and the Intensification of Class Struggle", *Journal of Peasant Studies,* 35/4: 557–620.

Watts, M. (2001): "1968 and All That ...", *Progress in Human Geography,* 25/2: 157–188.

Whitehead, J. (2003). "Space, Place and Primitive Accumulation in Narmada Valley and Beyond", *Economic and Political Weekly*, 38/40: 4224–4230.

Whitehead, J. (2012):"John Locke, Accumulation by Dispossession and the Governance of Colonial India", *Journal of Contemporary Asia*, 42/1: 1–21.

Williams, P., Vira, B. and Chopra, D. (2011): "Marginality, Agency and Power: Experiencing the State in Contemporary India", *Pacific Affairs*, 84/1: 7–23.

Williams, R. (1977): *Marxism and Literature*, Oxford: Oxford University Press.

Wolf, E.R. (1969): *Peasant Wars of the Twentieth Century*, New York: Harper and Row.

Wolf, E.R. (1982): *Europe and the People Without History*, Berkeley: University of California Press.

World Bank (2011): *Poverty and Social Exclusion in India*, Washington, D.C.: The World Bank.

Yadav, Y. (2000): "Understanding the Second Democratic Upsurge: Trends of Bahujan Participation in Electoral Politics in the 1990s", in Frankel, F.R., Hasan, Z., Bhargava, R. and Arora, B. (eds.): *Transforming India: Social and Political Dynamics of Democracy*, Oxford: Oxford University Press.

Index